# Going for Gold

## 2008 U.S. Women's Olympic Gymnastics

An Unauthorized Biography by Leigh Olsen

PSS!

PRICE STERN SLOAN

PRICE STERN SLOAN
Published by the Penguin Group
Penguin Group (USA) Inc., 375 Hudson Street, New York, New York 10014, USA
Penguin Group (Canada), 90 Eglinton Avenue East, Suite 700,
Toronto, Ontario M4P 2Y3, Canada
(a division of Pearson Penguin Canada Inc.)
Penguin Books Ltd., 80 Strand, London WC2R 0RL, England
Penguin Group Ireland, 25 St. Stephen's Green, Dublin 2, Ireland
(a division of Penguin Books Ltd.)
Penguin Group (Australia), 250 Camberwell Road, Camberwell, Victoria 3124, Australia
(a division of Pearson Australia Group Pty. Ltd.)
Penguin Books India Pvt. Ltd., 11 Community Centre, Panchsheel Park,
New Delhi—110 017, India
Penguin Group (NZ), 67 Apollo Drive, Rosedale, North Shore 0632, New Zealand
(a division of Pearson New Zealand Ltd.)
Penguin Books (South Africa) (Pty.) Ltd., 24 Sturdee Avenue,
Rosebank, Johannesburg 2196, South Africa

Penguin Books Ltd., Registered Offices:
80 Strand, London WC2R 0RL, England

*Photo credits:* Cover photos: courtesy of AP Photo/Rick Rycroft, AP Photo/Ann Heisenfelt,
AP Photo/Eric Risberg. Insert photos: first page courtesy of Evaristo Sa/AFP/Getty Images
(top photo), Chris Trotman/Stringer/Getty Images (bottom photo); second page courtesy of
Thomas Niedermueller/Stringer/Getty Images (top photo), courtesy of Luis Gene/AFP/Getty
Images (bottom photo); third page photo courtesy of Jed Jacobsohn/Getty Image; fourth
page courtesy of Luis Gene/AFP/Getty Images.

Library of Congress Control Number: 2008018005

ISBN 978-0-8431-3348-6          10 9 8 7 6 5 4 3 2 1

# Going for Gold

## 2008 U.S. Women's Olympic Gymnastics

An Unauthorized Biography by Leigh Olsen

PSS!
PRICE STERN SLOAN

# Table of Contents

# Table of Contents

# Introduction

## Fantastic Gymnastics

The stadium is packed with spectators. Vendors wander through the rows of seats selling T-shirts, banners, cotton candy, hot dogs, and sodas. Little girls eagerly wiggle around in their seats, trying to get a better view of the action down on the stadium floor. A hush falls over the crowd as a small girl wearing a sparkling red leotard steps out onto the floor. She takes a deep breath and positions herself in front of a long, narrow balance beam.

Tension is thick in the air. Then with a nod from the judges, she runs toward the beam and flips up onto it. She hits a high V with her arms and then performs a series of spins and jumps. The crowd oohs and aahs as she gracefully maneuvers on the thin beam, performing flips and tricks that stun spectators and judges alike. Then she pauses, just for a moment, and takes a deep breath. Everyone knows what's coming next. The crowd holds its breath as she gives them a dazzling smile and launches into a tumbling pass. Back handspring. Back handspring. Twisting full layout. She lands with her heels at the very edge of the beam, wobbling slightly.

The crowd gasps, on the edge of their seats. Will she fall? But she catches her balance and stands up straight with a nervous grin. She made it. The crowd sighs, leaning back. She performs a few more tumbling passes, each more impressive than the last. Finally she tumbles the length of the beam and flips off it, hitting the ground with her feet together and her arms up—a perfect landing. The crowd bursts into applause, whistling and cheering as the gymnast smiles and waves, thrilled with her performance. It was an almost flawless routine—but will it be enough for the gold? She would have been a shoo-in for first at some other gymnastics competitions, but this is the biggest gymnastics competition in the world—the Olympics—and here, anything can happen.

Every Olympic team is vying for the ultimate athletic honor—a shiny gold medal emblazoned with the famous five-ring logo. Every team wants to stand on the gold-medal podium, watch their country's flag being hoisted to the top of the flagpole, and listen as their country's national anthem blares throughout the stadium. Every team wants to bask in the glow of hundreds of flashbulbs and television cameras capturing this iconic moment—the moment their team receives team gold.

The pressure to win a medal at the Olympics is intense for every single team, but it's especially bad for the women's gymnastics teams. Women's gymnastics is one of the few Olympic sports made up entirely of teenage athletes. Most other girls their age are worrying about prom, the SATs, and getting their driver's licenses—but not these girls. These young women have the hopes and dreams of their entire country resting on their shoulders. That's a lot of responsibility, especially when you consider just how stiff the competition is. Anything can happen in the heat of Olympic competition. The team that wins the gold will be the team that can maintain their grace and poise under all of that pressure and scrutiny.

So which country will come away with the prize at the 2008 Summer Olympics? Will it be the Chinese, fighting for a win on their home turf? Will it be Romania or Russia, two frequent medal contenders? Or will it be the United States, the reigning world champions?

Every single girl on the American gymnastics team has dreamed about winning the gold since she was little. They've trained almost their entire lives and competed numerous times just to stand on the Olympic stage. Making the team is one of the most difficult things a gymnast will ever do. In years past, the best gymnasts in the United States have made costly mistakes at the Olympic Trials or at the selection camp, dashing their hopes of competing for their country. Big dreams just aren't enough to ensure a gymnast makes the team. The United States is picking from the best of the best, so to win a spot, a gymnast must be dedicated, talented, prepared, and as close to perfect as possible. And the 2008 selection process will be harder than ever. Never before have there been so many talented girls to choose from.

The United States has only won Olympic team gold once, at the 1996 Olympics in Atlanta, Georgia. But in 2007, the U.S. women won the team gold at the World Championships in Germany. It was their first team World Championships win off U.S. soil. Will these gymnasts achieve a similar feat in Beijing, winning Olympic gold outside the United States for the first time in history? One thing's for sure, these girls are determined to go for gold, and they'll give the Olympics everything they have to achieve it!

# Chapter 1

## Olympic Dreams

Long before the modern Olympics, over 2,500 years ago, people began practicing gymnastics in ancient Greece. In fact, gymnastics is one of the oldest sports in the world. Only men performed then—and they performed it naked! In fact, *gymnos* is Greek for *naked*. The word *gymnastics* literally translates to "exercising naked" in Greek.

Obviously, gymnastics was very different back then. There were no uneven bars and balance beams. The one competition they had that we have now was a version of the vault. But Greek men weren't vaulting over stationary vaulting tables—they were vaulting over bulls! That's right—real, live bulls! They would race toward a bull, grab it by the horns, and launch themselves onto its back or do flips over it!

The Greeks were really into physical fitness, and Greek men would spend entire days competing in gymnastics events in open-air stadiums. And the Greeks didn't just invent gymnastics; they also started the Olympics! Way back in 776 B.C., Olympic events consisted mostly of footraces. The winners received an olive wreath, a new home, lots of money, and a lifetime's worth of free meals! Today's Olympic athletes don't get nearly as much cool stuff! Back then, there were no women gymnasts. Women weren't even allowed inside the Olympic stadium. In fact, if a woman was found watching, she was punished by being tossed off a cliff!

The Olympics—and women's rights—have come a long way since then. After the Romans conquered Greece, there were no more Olympics for the next 1,500 years. But in the late 1800s, a French nobleman convinced fourteen countries, not including the United States, to revive the competition. In 1896, the first modern Olympics were held where the games were born: Athens, Greece.

Women still weren't allowed to compete, but gymnastics was included in the 1896 Olympics. The sport had changed drastically over the years. Instead of vaulting over bulls, men competed on the regular vault. They also competed in the same events that male gymnasts compete in today—horizontal bar, parallel bars, pommel horse, and rings. In addition to gymnastics, the Olympic athletes competed in just eight other sports that year. The games have gotten significantly more diverse since then, and now there are twenty-eight summer Olympic sports.

In 1928, women made their first appearance in the gymnastics competition. They performed the same events as men, but there were no individual or all-around competitions. The women competed only as a team until 1952, when the first individual competitions became part of the Olympics. By then, women's gymnastics had been heavily influenced by dance and ballet, and the sport had evolved to focus more on grace, form, and fluid movement than it had originally.

In 1936, the U.S. women's gymnastics team competed for the first time at the Olympics in Berlin. Back then, the United States wasn't the powerhouse team it is today. They managed to take bronze at the 1948 Olympic Games in London but didn't place again until they won the silver in the 1984 Olympic Games in Los Angeles. Up until the 1980s, all the big names in gymnastics came out of Eastern Europe. But gymnastics didn't actually get much press until the 1970s, when it became one of the most popular Olympic sports, thanks to a tiny girl from the Soviet Union.

Olga Korbut officially became the first world-famous gymnast and brought global recognition to the sport at the 1972 Olympics in Munich. Olga was seventeen and just 4' 11" when she walked onto the competition floor. That might sound like a typical gymnast in today's world, but at the time, she was considered extremely small. Olga shocked the world when she performed backflips on both the beam and the uneven bars. That had never been done in a gymnastics competition—men's or women's—before! Olga won gold for her performances on the beam and the floor exercise, and the Soviet Union took the team gold. After the Olympics, Olga became one of the most famous women in the world. She was nicknamed "the Munchkin of Munich," and she met the queen of England and Richard Nixon, the president of the United States at the time. Meanwhile, the International Federation of Gymnastics, also known as the FIG, the group that oversees international gymnastics competition, tried to ban backflips in competition because they were worried that the move was too dangerous and gymnasts might get injured performing it. But when Olga said she would not come back to gymnastics if the ban went through, the FIG stopped trying for the ban. After all, Olga had brought world recognition to the sport.

After Olga's appearance at the Olympics, the number of gymnastics gyms throughout the world multiplied by ten! Olga had single-handedly transformed the sport, and just four years later, at the 1976 Montreal Olympics, the gymnastics competition was full of backflipping, petite girls like Olga. One of those new girls would unseat Olga as the queen of the gymnastics world— Nadia Comaneci. In 1968, Nadia was discovered by Bela Karolyi, a now world-famous gymnastics coach. He spotted her when she was just six in her hometown in Romania, a country in Eastern Europe, doing cartwheels on her elementary school playground. Bela invited Nadia to be a student at his national gymnastics school, which trained all of the Romanian gymnasts.

By age thirteen, Nadia was the best gymnast in Europe. And at fourteen, she traveled to the 1976

Olympics in Montreal, Quebec. She impressed the judges with her flawless, complicated moves, but once she got on the uneven bars, Nadia did the unthinkable. She scored a perfect ten. At the time, all routines were scored out of ten, but no gymnast had ever achieved a perfect score before. In fact, a score of ten was so unimaginable that the scoreboards weren't equipped to show more than three digits. So when Nadia finished her routine, the score showed up as a 1.00 instead of a 10.00! The next night, Nadia scored a perfect ten again on the balance beam. Throughout the competition, she scored seven perfect tens, easily winning the all-around gold.

While Nadia Comaneci was nailing perfect scores in Montreal, a little eight-year-old American girl named Mary Lou Retton was watching from home in the United States. Mary Lou may not have known it at the time, but she was destined to be a world-renowned gymnast just like her hero Nadia. When she was little, Mary Lou was a tomboy with lots of energy. Her parents enrolled her in dance early on, but she soon transitioned into gymnastics. By the age of twelve, she was the best gymnast in her home state of West Virginia, and Mary Lou was looking for a coach who could help her get to the next Olympics.

That's when she began working with Nadia Comaneci's former coach, Bela Karolyi. Bela and his wife, Martha, had recently moved to the United States from Romania to start a gymnastics school in Texas. So Mary Lou headed to Houston to train at Bela's ranch. Not long after, Mary Lou's Olympic dream came true when she made it to the 1984 Olympics in Los Angeles, California. In the all-around competition, Mary Lou was giving a stellar performance, but she was trailing Romania's Ecaterina Szabo, a former student of Bela's, by 0.15 points in the all-around competition. But Mary Lou still had to compete in floor and vault. She knew she needed to do the nearly impossible to win—she had to score perfect tens in both events. Mary Lou made it happen, nailing both routines, getting two tens in a row, and winning the all-around competition. She was the first American gymnast in history to win an Olympic medal in gymnastics! And it wasn't just any medal—it was the coveted gold. Mary Lou soared to fame, becoming the first female athlete to appear on the front of a box of Wheaties cereal, which was and still is a huge honor!

Mary Lou Retton put American gymnastics on the map. But the United States still hadn't won team gold at the Olympics. In 1996, that changed. The Magnificent Seven team of the 1996 Atlanta Olympics consisted of all-stars Shannon Miller, Dominique Dawes, Dominique Moceanu, Kerri Strug, Amy Chow, Amanda Borden, and Jaycie Phelps. Shannon Miller had already won five Olympic medals in the 1992 Barcelona Olympics, more than any other American gymnast had ever received. Dominique Dawes and Kerri Strug had also been on the 1992 team, which won the team silver medal. Bela Karolyi was back at the Olympics yet again, this time as the personal coach of Kerri Strug and Dominique Moceanu.

The Americans were in the lead in the team finals, but then Dominique Moceanu fell on both of her vaults and Kerri Strug fell on her first vault, injuring her ankle. The United States' chance at gold was in jeopardy. Kerri knew she had to nail her second vault to secure the team gold—even though she had torn two ligaments in her ankle on her first attempt. In one of the most memorable moments in Olympic history, Kerri nailed her vault—landing on just one foot! It was just what the team needed. The United States team had officially won their first gold medal, inspiring girls across the country to get into gymnastics, just like the Magnificent Seven.

Today, there are several ways for girls to become elite, or Olympic-level, gymnasts. Many begin competing in the Talent Opportunity Program, or TOPs. TOPs seeks out gymnasts between the ages of seven and eleven, evaluating them on their strength and flexibility. Each year, TOPs tests gymnasts on basic gymnastics skills, and the top two gymnasts in the nation are awarded a trip to an elite training camp.

Lots of elite gymnasts also get their start in the Junior Olympics program. The Junior Olympics, an entirely separate program from TOPs, has ten levels. Girls can start as early as four years old in the program at level one, rising through the ranks as they improve in skill level. Competitions are held at local, state, regional, and national levels, though you must be a level nine or ten to compete in Nationals. A gymnast must be at least nine years old to be in level ten. After reaching level ten, a Junior Olympic gymnast may test to be a junior national elite gymnast, which is the lowest elite level. A gymnast doesn't have to be in the Junior Olympics program to test, but most are. Any gymnast can test for the elite levels. If a gymnast qualifies for junior international elite, she can compete at elite competitions within the United States. A junior national elite gymnast may eventually qualify for international competition, making her a junior international elite. Finally, she must progress to the senior elite level before she can make the Olympic team. A gymnast has to turn at least sixteen during her first year as a senior elite to be allowed to compete at that level.

Whether it's three-year-olds in their first gymnastics class or senior elites competing on the international stage, gymnastics has come a long way since ancient Greece. Every year gymnastics competitions become more and more difficult as new gymnasts perform innovative tricks and bring a fresh perspective to the sport. One thing's for sure: The world will be watching and waiting with bated breath to see what the 2008 games will bring.

# Chapter 2

## All-Around Awesome

There is no greater honor in gymnastics than to be awarded a gold medal in the all-around competition. To win that coveted first-place spot, gymnasts must receive high scores in all four of the women's events. They are, in order of competition, the vault, the uneven bars, the balance beam, and the floor exercise. Each of the events showcases different skills and abilities. The vault allows a gymnast to show off her strength; she can demonstrate her grace and agility on the uneven bars; the balance beam requires a gymnast to be poised and focused under pressure; and the floor routine is for demonstrating showmanship. Lots of gymnasts will receive high scores in one or two events, but it is a rare gymnast who gets top marks in all four.

### Vault

In vault, gymnasts must run down a long pathway, jump off a springboard and onto the "horse," do an impressive series of acrobatic elements, and then land solidly. This event is difficult because it requires an incredible amount of strength and speed. The best vaulters are usually the strongest gymnasts, and they usually have more muscle tone and stockier builds.

During the run-up portion, a gymnast races as fast as

she can down the eighty-two-foot runway. Top gymnasts might reach speeds of up to seventeen miles per hour! The faster a gymnast runs, the more power she has to push off the springboard and onto the vault. Gymnasts don't usually cover the entire eighty-two-foot runway. They have a starting point, depending on how many steps they know they'll make on the way to the springboard. Top gymnasts always have a set number of steps that they take before vaulting. In fact, if a gymnast realizes while she's running that she's off on her number of steps, she can veer off the runway and start over.

Once the gymnast makes it down the runway, she jumps onto the springboard. The springboard is a two-by-four-foot platform with thick springs inside. Using both feet, the gymnast launches herself off the springboard so that she's flying headfirst toward the horse. A gymnast usually enters a vault by doing a handspring or a round-off on the runway, landing with her feet on the springboard, and pushing off into the vault.

The gymnast then lands with her hands on the horse, which is forty-seven inches off the ground, and pushes off the horse and into her vault, trying to get as much height as possible. The best vaulters can fling themselves over eight feet into the air! Judges pay attention to how high a gymnast goes and how far she travels through the air.

Once a gymnast has pushed off the horse, she has a chance to show off by performing a series of elements in the air. The gymnast might vault in the tucked, pike, or layout position. A tuck is when a gymnast's arms and legs are tucked into her body; a pike is when the gymnast's legs are straight, with her arms reaching toward her toes; and a layout is when the gymnast's body is completely straight. The gymnast will do as many saltos (somersaults) or twists as possible in one of these positions. Legs must be together, with toes pointed. Generally, the more saltos and twists, the higher she will be scored.

Finally, the gymnast must "stick" her landing. This means that the gymnast has to make a landing cleanly, with her feet a few inches apart, trying not to hop or take any steps. She can bend her knees a little, but not too much. Since the landing is the last thing the judges see, it's got to be good to leave a positive impression. Sticking a landing can make or break a routine in every event—and it often does. If two gymnasts each perform practically perfect routines, but one of the gymnasts moves one foot even the tiniest bit in her landing, the girl who sticks her landing will win.

The vault event lasts for approximately five seconds from takeoff to landing. This means that throughout the performance, the gymnast has to be incredibly focused.

Famous vaults include the Yurchenko and the Tsukahara, both named after the gymnasts who invented them. In the Yurchenko, invented by Natalia Yurchenko of Russia, the gymnast enters the vault with a round-off and does double twists off the horse. In the Tsukahara, named for male gymnast Mitsuo Tsukahara of Japan, the gymnast does a quarter-turn round-off entry and a back salto off the horse.

## The Uneven Bars

Crowds love to watch gymnasts perform on the uneven bars, and it is possibly the most popular event. In this event, gymnasts perform a series of acrobatic stunts while swinging around and between two bars of uneven heights. Gymnasts flow seamlessly from one movement to the next, using both of the bars. Their bodies are completely straight when in the vertical position—like when they hit handstands, for example—but fluid and flexible as they move to other elements.

The high bar is eight feet off the ground and the low bar is five and a half feet off the ground. The gymnast will perform release moves, in which she goes from one bar to the other or releases the bar only to regrasp the same bar again. Release moves are the most daring part of the routine since the gymnasts have to be very precise. When a gymnast is switching from bar to bar, she doesn't want to use too much strength in her release since it might throw off her routine. She also can't use too little strength since she might miss the bar altogether and fall, ruining her performance. A gymnast is allowed only five moves in a row on one bar before she must switch to the other bar, and she has to perform at least two release moves in her routine, although usually she'll do more than that.

The gymnast also must complete at least ten continuous moves in her routine, which lasts only thirty seconds. Judges don't want to see any pauses between movements. Everything should be seamless. The gymnast must change directions and use different types of holds on the bar, as she is constantly in motion. At the end of her routine, she dismounts using a series of somersaults and twists, and, of course, she should stick her landing.

Most gymnasts use special hand grips during this event. Each grip is a leather strap that fits over the palm of the hand, fastening at the wrist. These grips help to protect gymnasts from tearing the delicate skin of their hands on the bars, although even the grips can't completely stop this from happening. To further reduce friction and protect their skin, gymnasts "chalk up" right before this event by rubbing chalk on their hands and feet.

## The Balance Beam

Many gymnasts think that the balance beam is the most difficult event. After all, they have to stand four feet off the ground, doing turns and jumps and flips on a four-inch-wide beam. It's hard enough to perform those moves on the ground! It's also nearly impossible to cover up a mistake on the beam. If someone is even the tiniest bit off balance, it will show with an obvious wobble, which will cause her to lose points. And if she falls, she automatically loses 0.80 points off her score. That's a lot of pressure to stay focused!

Judges begin scoring a gymnast when she mounts the beam. A gymnast may either mount the beam by running and jumping onto it, by hoisting herself onto it from a standing position, or by jumping onto it with a springboard. The more difficult the mount, the more points the gymnast receives. For example, flipping onto the beam after jumping off a springboard is worth more points than pushing up onto the beam from a standing position.

In competitions, a gymnast has to complete five requirements on the beam. First of all, a routine must be between seventy and ninety seconds long. A minute and a half may not seem like much time, but when a gymnast is doing such careful work on such a small surface, just staying on the beam for that length of time is a big challenge! As in the uneven bars, judges like to see continuous movement on the beam—that means no stopping to take a deep breath before an especially difficult move.

One of the strangest requirements of the beam is that a gymnast has to cover the entire length of the six-foot beam during the course of the routine. Most girls achieve this by landing a tumbling sequence with their heels right at the very end of the beam. Usually, a girl will cover the length of the beam at least six times throughout her routine with a combination of dance and acrobatic moves. A gymnast must also perform at least one three-hundred-and-sixty-degree turn on one foot. And she must complete a backward and a forward or sideways acrobatic element, like a walkover, cartwheel, handspring, or roll.

Finally, every balance beam routine must include acrobatic and dance series of two or more combined elements. An acrobatic series might consist of a back handspring followed by a back salto. A dance series could be a split jump followed by a turn, a leap in which the gymnast's legs form a one-hundred-and-eighty-degree line. When a gymnast has completed her routine, she must dismount the beam. She will usually perform a series and then flip off the beam, sticking the landing.

### The Floor Exercise

The floor exercise is the only gymnastics event set to music, and it combines dance and tumbling for an exciting, energetic performance. The music cannot contain lyrics or spoken words, but otherwise it can be any genre, so there is always a lot of variety in the floor exercise. The crowd often gets into the routine by clapping and cheering along, providing energy that can really help a gymnast through her routine. It's the one event where a gymnast gets the opportunity to really express herself and where the judges score her higher if she does!

The floor routine showcases a gymnast's

showmanship and athletic ability. Some of the things these young women can accomplish seem to defy the laws of gravity! Kim Zmeskal, a star in the 1992 Olympics, could do a round-off into a triple whip back, which is three backflips in a row—all with no hands! The best gymnasts make extremely difficult elements like these look completely effortless.

The floor itself is forty square feet of plywood covered by two inches of padding and blue cloth set on top of four-inch springs or foam padding. This floor is a little bouncy, which protects gymnasts' joints when they perform high-impact moves. Until the mid-1960s, the floor routine was performed on much more dangerous surfaces like a hard wooden floor or on a floor covered in canvas, with no padding whatsoever! The floor is usually brightly colored, making it easy for a gymnast to tell if she has stepped out-of-bounds. Staying within the floor's boundaries is part of the challenge, and a gymnast will be docked points if she steps out-of-bounds.

The floor exercise runs seventy to ninety seconds long, and it usually includes four or five tumbling passes, made up of a series of tumbling elements. Popular elements include triple twists, double-twisting layout fronts, and double Arabians, in which a gymnast twists into a double salto and lands facing the opposite direction. To excel at this event, a gymnast must have powerful tumbling skills and she must get an impressive distance off the ground during each move. Gymnasts usually perform their most difficult tumbling pass first, when they have the most energy. Dance elements include leaps and turns, which keep the routine lively and exciting. Overall, a gymnast should showcase her grace and flexibility in her floor routine.

The floor exercise is difficult because the gymnast has to have incredible stamina to keep on bouncing through her routine with a consistent amount of energy. As with the balance beam, ninety seconds may not seem like such a long time, but after performing all of the acrobatics that go into a floor routine, anyone would be exhausted!

## Scoring

The Beijing 2008 Summer Olympics are the first Olympic Games to use a brand-new scoring system. Until 2006, gymnastics was based on a ten-point scale. With the old system, judges determined a gymnast's "start value" before she performed her routine based on the elements she told them would be in her routine. Then, as she performed, points were deducted for mistakes in execution or if a gymnast left out an element. Each female gymnast started out with a 9.0 for completing all the basic elements of a routine. Then she could be awarded up to one bonus point for completing additional, more difficult moves so that the total possible score was 10.0. So if a gymnast's routine included all of the basic elements plus two slightly more challenging moves, then her start value might be a 9.5. If she performed the routine flawlessly, then she would be awarded a 9.5, but if she messed up a few times, she might receive a 9.2. The very best gymnasts always made sure that their routines had a start value of 10.0 so that they had the potential to get a perfect score. Fans knew that when a score near ten popped on their screen, a gymnast had done an almost perfect job.

The scoring system was changed because of a controversy after the 2004 Athens Olympics men's gymnastics finals. At Athens, bronze medalist Yang Tae-Young of South Korea was wrongly docked a tenth of a point, and because of that, he lost the all-around gold to the United States' Paul Hamm by just 0.049. After that debacle, the FIG reevaluated the scoring system. In the new system, there is no maximum score. Gymnasts receive two scores: an execution score, which is out of ten points, and a difficulty score, which is open-ended. Deductions for faults in execution, technique, and artistry or composition are taken out of the 10.0 execution score, while the difficulty score acts more like bonus points. It is added to the execution score, but no deductions are taken from it for mistakes. So now, a gymnast could, in theory, score as high as a 20.0 or a 30.0, although no one has scored that high yet! The new system is supposed to help gymnasts whose difficulty levels exceed those of other gymnasts.

So don't be shocked when a gymnast receives above a ten at the 2008 Olympics. A 15.6 doesn't mean that a gymnast has received extra credit—it's just the product of the new scoring system. Your best bet for figuring out just how well a gymnast has performed is to compare her score to the others received in the same event. Generally, scores in the fifteen to sixteen range are very good. And don't forget to factor in the cheering of the crowd—always a good indicator that a gymnast has nailed her routine!

# Chapter 3

## Global Conquest

Every gymnastics meet is important to the gymnasts who compete. Getting the chance to show off in front of judges, fans, and fellow athletes is what gymnasts live for, but one meet in particular overshadows the rest every year—the World Championships. Worlds provide gymnasts the opportunity to compete on the global stage and to check out the competition from around the globe. It's always interesting and exciting for American gymnast to see the innovative routines that come out of Brazil, Russia, China, and Japan. The fierce competition always inspires gymnasts to do their very best, and every four years, Worlds takes on special significance as a preview of what fans will see at the Olympics.

The U.S. Women's Gymnastics Team competing at the 2007 World Championships in Stuttgart, Germany, consisted of superstars Shawn Johnson, Nastia Liukin, Alicia Sacramone, Samantha Peszek, Shayla Worley, Ivan Hong, and alternate Bridget Sloan. The girls had been training rigorously, and they walked into the competition ready to dominate. They started things out with a bang, finishing first in the qualification round, which moved them forward to the team finals round. Team coordinator Martha Karolyi told usa-gymnastics.org, "I really liked the way these young girls went out there tonight, and you must remember they are a very young team. They showed confidence out there today. I have faith in them."

It was an especially awesome day for Shayla Worley, who was not only celebrating the team's first-day results, but also her seventeenth birthday! "There's no better gift than to be able to compete at a World Championships on your birthday," Shayla told *ABC News*. "Well, maybe competing at the Olympics. We'll have to work on that for next year." Unfortunately for Shayla, the day wasn't totally perfect. She and Shawn Johnson had both fallen during their uneven bars dismounts in preliminaries. But the team stayed positive, and both girls resolved to do better in finals. Shawn told usa-gymnastics.org, "We came out so strong as a team, and we set the bar so high. We made a few mistakes, but we are going to go back and work a little harder for finals."

Shawn wasn't kidding! The U.S. performance in team finals began strongly, and they took an early lead, just slightly ahead of China, after the vault and uneven bars. But once the team rotated to the balance beam, things fell apart. In the team finals, each team sends its three strongest gymnasts in each event to compete in that event, so not everyone performs in every event.

On balance beam, Nastia Liukin performed her routine almost flawlessly—until the end. During her dismount, Nastia's footing was off. To save herself from falling, she scaled back her two-and-a-half twist dismount to a simple back tuck dismount, which is a basic beginner gymnastics skill. "I think I just rushed too early," Nastia told *ABC News*. "I did a good beam routine and I guess I just got too excited too early. I felt like my foot slipped, and I knew I wasn't going to able to complete the twist."

Shawn Johnson was up next on beam, but her performance didn't go any better than Nastia's. When she didn't land a series, she lost her balance and fell off the beam! Finally, Alicia Sacramone was up. Alicia put up the best performance of the three. But it wasn't enough to keep the United States ahead of China. They had fallen 0.10 points behind.

With just the floor routine to go, the United States was under immense pressure to pull out on top. The girls rallied together, as Nastia told *USA Today*: "Shawn was like, 'Only one-tenth, guys.' We were all really worked up. After she said that, we said, 'Okay, it's still possible. Don't give up, keep fighting, you're right there.'" Alicia, the team captain, gave the girls a pep talk and tried to get everyone psyched up for their last event. "I told them, 'Everyone makes mistakes, but we still have one more event and it's one of our best events, so we might as well go out there and have fun and show everybody what we've got. This is what we came to do,'" Alicia explained to the *Washington Post*.

Shayla and Shawn were up first on floor, with Alicia last. Shayla got them off to a great start with a solid performance that warmed up the crowd. "It was crazy," Shayla told usa-gymnastics.org. "We made some mistakes [before floor], but we knew it wasn't too late. It was the most pressure I have ever had in my life, but it felt great to go out and do it." Then Shawn came out, wowing the judges with her high-flying tumbling passes and her ear-to-ear grin. "I knew I brought us down a little bit on beam. I knew I had to go out and perform and redeem ourselves and redeem the team," Shawn told *ABC News*.

When Shawn finished up her routine, the rest of the U.S. team was screaming and cheering. They knew she'd done well, and she had! Shawn's awesome 15.375 put the team back into contention for the top spot. It was all up to Alicia, and she needed to score higher than 14.375 to nab the team gold medal. "It was a lot of pressure to put on myself," Alicia told *ABC News*. "All the girls were like, 'You can do it,' and, 'It's fine.' I was like, 'Guys, c'mon, I'm fine.'" Alicia was more than just fine. She blew the roof off the house with her flashy, solid routine.

Even before Alicia had finished, Martha Karolyi was jumping up and down on the sidelines. She knew the team had just secured the gold medal. Alicia told usa-gymnastics.org, "It was a little nerve-racking to see the mistakes the others made, and as the last routine, I knew I could get a big score."

The United States had done it—they were the 2007 world champions! "We all started crying," Nastia told

*ABC News*. "It's such a great feeling to know that finally we're on top of the world again." Her teammates completely agreed. "It was a great week," Alicia told usa-gymnastics.org. "We came and did what we set out to do, to win the title. To win [the team title] at World Championships outside the U.S.A. is really an achievement. I believe we left a good impression heading into the Olympic year." What made their achievement even more special was that it marked the first time the U.S. team had won the gold at a World Championships held outside the United States. The girls had made history.

Aside from achieving world champion status, the team had become close friends over the course of the competition. They had really come together. "I will never forget how great we all bonded and became such good friends," Ivana Hong told usa-gymnastics.org. "While gone from home, they were the only family we had and so we all became really close." Even with all the hard work and all the pressure, the girls had found plenty of time for laughter and fun. "We had such good times, and there are so many inside jokes we shared. You don't realize all of that stuff until you get home and try to say them to someone else, and they look at you like you're crazy and you're like, 'I guess no one knows what I'm talking about. I'll stop talking now.' We all got really close over there. I miss that the most," Alicia told *NBC Sports*. Samantha Peszek told usa-gymnastics.org that the hardest part was saying good-bye. "Our team chemistry was so great and we worked so well together. Although I wanted to come home at the end of the trip, I was sad to leave all the girls." At least they were leaving one another on a high note—with the promise of more competitions together in the future.

As Martha Karolyi told *ABC News* after Worlds, "I already gave the message to the team: This is not the end of the road, this is the beginning of the road." The U.S. win at the World Championships was a great start down the path to Olympic gold in Beijing, and one thing's for sure—the United States team will have confidence on their side when they arrive in China. "We're going to the Olympic Games as world champions," Nastia told the *Washington Post*. "How much better can you feel?"

# Chapter 4

## World Champions

The United States has some of the top women gymnasts in the world—and they've got the proof: a team gold medal from the 2007 World Championships! Very few gymnasts can claim to be world champions, which makes these women extra special.

The 2007 U.S. team competing at the World Championships included seven girls: Shawn Johnson, Nastia Liukin, Alicia Sacramone, Samantha Peszek, Shayla Worley, Ivana Hong, and an alternate, Bridget Sloan. Here's an up-close and personal look at the champs:

---

**To keep up with the fast-paced events at the Olympics, here are the key abbreviations you'll need to know!**

**AA:** All-around
**FX:** Floor Exercise
**UB:** Uneven Bars
**BB:** Balance Beam
**VT:** Vault
**T:** Tie

---

# SHAWN JOHNSON

**Full Name:** Shawn Machel Johnson
**Nickname:** Peanut
**Date of Birth:** January 19, 1992
**Hometown:** Des Moines, Iowa
**Height:** 4' 8"
**Eye Color:** Light blue
**Hair Color:** Dark blond
**Official Website:** www.shawnjohnson.net
**Favorite Event:** Balance beam
**Senior Elite Medals:**

2008 Tyson American Cup: 2nd-AA

2008 Italy-Spain-Poland-USA competition: 1st-Team, AA

2007 World Championships: 1st-Team, AA, FX; 8th-BB

2007 Pan American Games: 1st-Team, AA, UB, BB; 2nd-FX

2007 Tyson American Cup: 1st-AA

2007 USA vs. Great Britain International Competition:
  1st-Team, AA, BB; 2nd-VT

2007 Visa Championships: 1st-AA, BB, FX; 3rd-UB

2006 International Gymnix: 3rd-AA; 2nd-VT; 5th-UB; 1st-FX

2006 USA/Japan/New Zealand Competition: 1st-AA, VT, BB;
  3rd-UB; 2nd-FX

2005 Top Gym Competition: 1st-AA, VT, FX

## Shawn's Early Years

When Shawn was born, she had no heart rate! Baby
Shawn was technically dead at birth, but luckily doctors

were able to resuscitate her. After Shawn's condition stabilized, her parents, Doug and Teri, took their firstborn daughter home. For someone who had been born so weak, Shawn surprised everyone by growing into a very energetic toddler.

As a baby, "she never bothered to crawl," Shawn's mother, Teri, explained to *ABC News*. Instead, Shawn managed to climb out of her crib and simply *walk* right into her parents' bedroom! They couldn't believe their eyes when they saw their daughter standing there. "She started walking when she was nine months old and never slowed down," Teri continued. Considering that most kids don't learn to walk until they're at least a year old, Shawn's parents knew right away that she was going places!

When she was three years old, Shawn, an only child, had so much energy that she desperately needed an outlet. Her parents tried taking her to dance classes, but even that wasn't enough. "She wasn't that well behaved," Teri told *USA Today*. "She was just everywhere." That's when the idea of gymnastics occurred to Shawn's parents. They enrolled her at a local gymnastics class to burn off her energy. Shawn adored gymnastics and wanted to compete, but her coach was not impressed with her potential. Shawn told *Inside Gymnastics* magazine online, "I don't know what happened with the coach there, but he just said I was a little girl full of a lot of strength, but not a lot of talent. People can have their own opinions, but it wasn't something my parents wanted to hear. My parents didn't know if that coach was right for me, so we looked for a new one."

## Finding a Coach

Shawn found the perfect coaches for her, Liang Chow and Liwen Zhuang, at Chow's Gymnastics, a newly opened gym in Des Moines. Liang told *Inside Gymnastics*, "Shawn and her mom walked in, and she was six years old. She jumped right on the bars and swung like a monkey and was just a happy camper. You could tell this kid just loved gymnastics." Shawn and her new coaches were a match made in gymnastics heaven, and they've been working together ever since.

After seven years of training together, Liang saw such potential in Shawn that he wrote a letter to Martha Karolyi, national team coordinator of the U.S. Women's Gymnastics Team and wife of famous gymnastics coach Bela Karolyi. In the letter, Liang told Martha that he believed one of his gymnasts could be an asset to the U.S. team. Liang also enclosed a tape of some of Shawn's gymnastics highlights. Martha liked what she saw, and in no time, thirteen-year-old Shawn joined the U.S. team at the junior level.

## Joining the U.S. Gymnastics Team

From her first competition as a member of the U.S.

team, Shawn set out to impress. She drew national attention at the U.S. Classic in 2005, placing third all-around in the junior division. Then the following year, she placed first all-around at the National Championships. Although she was still competing at the junior level, Shawn scored better than senior-level gymnasts Chellsie Memmel, the 2005 world champion, and Nastia Liukin, a two-time national champion.

Shawn's gymnastics career was on fire, and by 2007 she was competing alongside Chellsie, Nastia, and the rest of the senior-level gymnasts. That's when Shawn really began to shine. In 2007, she placed first all-around at every competition she took part in! The first was at the USA vs. Great Britain International Competition in Ireland. The second was at the 2007 American Cup, her first international competition. "It was amazing. Hearing the crowd made me want to do so much better, and it really pumped me up," Shawn told gymnasticsmedia.com. She also won first at the Pan American Games, and finally, she won at Nationals, securing her spot on the U.S. World Championship team.

### The Worlds

At the World gymnastics competition in Germany, Shawn nailed almost every performance and left the competition with yet another all-around gold medal—but this time, she was world champion. Shawn was only the fourth American woman to win that title, along with teammate Chellsie Memmel and former U.S. team members Shannon Miller and Shawn's idol, Kim Zmeskal. But Shawn didn't bask in the glow of her personal glory; the best part for her was the team's win. Shawn told *USA Gymnastics*, "We had been working together as a team for so long that when we finally got ahold of that gold medal, nothing in the world could have felt better. We hugged and cried and just really shared the moment as a true team."

## Media Frenzy

After Worlds, Shawn received another very prestigious honor, the Longines Prize for Elegance, which consisted of five thousand dollars, a luxury wristwatch, and a cool trophy. The award goes to the gymnast with the most charm, beauty, grace, and charisma in competition every year. Shawn sure has all of those qualities—and then some! Meanwhile, people were beginning to speculate that Shawn was a shoo-in for the Olympic team in 2008. She did hit a snag in her plans when she sustained a minor injury in training, suffering a stress reaction in her right shin, but even that didn't slow her down. And as Shawn would soon find out, things were *really* about to pick up speed.

First, Governor Chet Culver named October 17, 2007, Shawn Johnson Day in Iowa. That's right. Shawn had a whole day devoted to her! In his speech that day, Governor Culver said, "Shawn Johnson is a role model for thousands of girls in Iowa and millions more around the country and the world. I am proud that she represents herself, her family, her state, and her nation with grace and dignity. We wish her the best of luck as she heads to Beijing, China, for the 2008 Summer Olympics." Even Shawn was blown away. "It was a really meaningful day," she said to *Inside Gymnastics*. "To have a day named [in your honor] is pretty crazy." And that was just the beginning of a few whirlwind months.

For starters, Shawn was named *ABC News'* Person of the Week. Then she appeared on *Ellen*, where she performed a routine on the uneven bars after her interview. Shawn told *Inside Gymnastics*, "Ellen was really nice . . . She wanted to learn some gymnastics, but I think her back was hurting, so we didn't get to do that." Then Shawn was invited to appear on *Access Hollywood*, where the interviewer asked her who her celebrity crushes are. Her answers? Lance Armstrong of Tour de France fame and Channing Tatum of *Step Up*. "I'd love to meet him," Shawn gushed about Channing.

Shawn was also a presenter at ABC's televised event "Frosted Pink," an initiative to raise awareness about women's cancers. Shawn's grandmother Gloria is a cancer survivor, so the cause hit close to home. It was at "Frosted Pink" that she got to meet her all-time favorite band, Rascall Flatts. "I couldn't believe I got to meet them. I still can't believe it!" Shawn told *Inside*

*Gymnastics*. "They were great and a lot of fun. They wanted me to teach them some gymnastics! It's crazy. I mean, they are my favorite music group, and it was just a really exciting moment." Shawn was basking in the glow of the spotlight, too. "I love the attention," Shawn told *Inside Gymnastics*, "and I think it helps my performance. It encourages me to want to do better."

## Endorsements

While Shawn was busy being a media darling, the endorsement deals started rolling in. Left and right, companies approached Shawn to be the face of their advertising campaigns during the 2008 Olympics. Eventually, she signed on with big names like Coca-Cola and Adidas. Advertisers loved her winning smile and spunky personality, so she was perfect to get attention for their products. Shawn's New York agent, Sheryl Shade, was also the agent for Shannon Miller and other members of the 1996 Magnificent Seven gymnastics team, which graced the Wheaties box after their Olympic win. But the attention Shawn is getting surpasses even that of the 1996 team. "I've never seen a gymnast get this much interest prior to the games. It's a little unbelievable, to tell you the truth," Sheryl told the *Des Moines Business Record*.

Because Shawn is getting paid for working with advertisers, she is no longer considered an amateur athlete. Instead, she has "gone pro," which means she can't join a gymnastics team in college or be eligible for a gymnastics scholarship to attend college. But as Shawn told the *Des Moines Business Record*, going pro was "honestly the best decision of my life." Shawn's mom, Teri, said to the *Des Moines Business Record*, "I felt there would be so many more opportunities for her future going this way, and she will probably have a much wider range of college options, also. I like the idea of her choosing a college for the school rather than their gymnastics program." As in every other area of her life, Shawn has set big goals for herself for college. She plans to use her endorsement money to study medicine at an Ivy League university like Harvard, Yale, or Princeton. She has always wanted to be a doctor, and she is also thinking about becoming a sports commentator, like Shannon Miller is today.

## Just a Regular Girl

Shawn certainly has the smarts to do whatever she wants. She is currently on the honor roll with a perfect 4.0 grade point average at Valley Southwoods High School, where she just finished tenth grade. But she keeps a low profile at school. "It's pretty much like two completely different lives, gym and school," Shawn told nbcolympics.com. "I don't really talk much about [gymnastics] life to them. It doesn't really mix that much. I've never been that kind of person to brag about it or anything—they read it in newspapers or see on

TV. I don't really say much. They congratulate me, but that's about it. I'm a normal person at school, a normal teenager." It's unusual for gymnasts at Shawn's level to attend regular public school, but somehow, she balances it all.

During her sophomore year, a typical day for Shawn included getting up at 6:00 A.M. to finish her homework and get ready for school, where she took geometry, French, biology, and American literature. She says her favorite subject is English, but her best subject is math. Then after school, she went to the gym to train for four hours. When Shawn appeared on *Ellen*, she said that's actually *less* time than average for a gymnast of her level, but that she manages to fit in just as much work. "Most girls my level will go six to eight hours at least. I don't know, I guess our workouts are different. Really, once you get in there, you don't stop. You get five minutes for a break, and that's about it."

## The Complete Package

Shawn Johnson really does have it all: talent, personality, and one of the strongest work ethics in the business. Her hard work is paying off, and she's getting praise from some of the biggest names in gymnastics. "She is the whole package," Mary Lou Retton said to *NBC Sports*. "She has the talent. She has the flair. She's got the personality . . . I definitely think America is ready for her." Shannon Miller thinks Shawn's got the right stuff, too. "You can be a powerful gymnast and not be top in the world. You can be a graceful gymnast and not be top in the world. You have to have that combination of the two," Shannon told sports.yahoo.com. "I think she has that and the crowd loves her. She's actually out there having fun. She's enjoying it and that comes through from the inside out. It's a breath of fresh air." Shawn has even impressed the person whose opinion matters the most in the U.S. women's gymnastics world: Martha Karolyi. "She certainly brings world-level gymnastics," Martha said to *USA Today*, adding, "We are expecting a very strong showing of this young gymnast."

In her short four years on the U.S. team, Shawn has wowed gymnastics insiders and observers alike. They are convinced—this tiny girl from Iowa is headed for success. Shawn joked to gymnasticsmedia.com that were she not a gymnast, she might change one small thing about her life: "I would probably be a little taller than I am." But Shawn's fans are glad she isn't taller. This little ball of energy is perfect just the way she is, and she's poised for an incredible gymnastics future.

# NASTIA LIUKIN

**Full Name:** Anastasia Valeryevna Liukin
**Nickname:** Nastia
**Date of Birth:** October 30, 1989
**Hometown:** Moscow, Russia
**Height:** 5' 2"
**Eye Color:** Blue
**Hair Color:** Blond
**Official Website:** www.nastialiukin.com
**Favorite Event:** Uneven bars, Balance beam
**Senior Elite Medals:**

2008 Tyson American Cup: 1st-AA

2007 World Championships: 1st-Team, BB; 2nd-UB; 5th-AA

2007 Pan American Games: 1st-Team; 2nd-UB, BB

2007 Visa Championships: 1st-UB; 2nd-BB; 3rd-AA; 12th-FX

2006 World Championships: 2nd-Team, UB

2006 Pacific Alliance Championships: 1st-Team, AA(T), UB; 2nd-BB

2006 Tyson American Cup: 1st-AA

2006 Visa Championships: 1st-AA, BB, UB; 7th-FX

2006 U.S. Classic: 1st-BB; 4th-AA; 6th-UB; 9th-VT(T), FX

2005 World Championships: 1st-UB, BB; 2nd-AA, FX

2005 USA/SUI: 1st-Team, AA, UB, BB, FX; 2nd-VT

2005 USA/GBR: 1st-Team, AA, BB, FX(T); 2nd-UB

2005 American Cup: 1st-BB(T); 6th-UB

2005 Visa Championships: 1st-AA, UB, BB; 2nd-FX

2005 U.S. Classic: 1st-AA, UB, BB; 2nd-FX; 4th-VT

2004 Visa Championships: 1st-AA, UB, BB, FX; 4th-VT
(Jr. Div.)

2004 American Classic: 1st-AA, BB, FX, UB (Jr. Div.)

2004 Pacific Alliance Championships: 1st-Team, AA, UB, BB,
FX (Jr. Div.)

2003 Pan American Games: 1st-Team, BB; 2nd-AA; 3rd-UB, FX

2003 National Championships: 1st-AA, UB, BB, FX (Jr. Div.)

2003 U.S. Classic: 1st-AA, VT, UB, BB, FX (Jr. Div.)

2003 American Classic: 1st-AA, FX; 2nd-UB (Jr. Div.)

2003 Podium Meet: 1st-AA, UB, BB, FX (Jr. Div.)

2002 USA/Canada: 1st-Team; 2nd-UB, FX; 3rd-AA, BB
(Jr. Div.)

2002 Junior Pan American Championships: 1st-Team; 2nd-AA,
UB, BB

2002 USA/Japan Dual Meet: 1st-Team, AA, UB, BB, FX

2002 U.S. Championships, Cleveland, Ohio: 5th-BB, FX
(Jr. Div.)

2002 U.S. Classic: 2nd-BB; 3rd-AA; 4th-FX, UB

2002 American Classic: 3rd-FX; 5th-BB

2002 Podium Meet: 5th-FX

## Gymnastics Genetics

Looking at her family's history, it seems like Nastia
Liukin was destined to be a star gymnast. Her father,
Valeri, won four medals for the Soviet Union gymnastics
team—two gold and two silver—at the 1988 Olympics.
He met Nastia's mother, Anna, the 1987 world champion
rhythmic gymnast, on a Soviet Union gymnastics tour

in Australia. But when Anastasia Valeryevna Liukin was born in Moscow, Russia, on October 30, 1989, a gymnastics career was the last thing her parents had in mind for her. "I don't even think they even wanted me to do [gymnastics] because they've been through it and because it's a really hard sport," Nastia, an only child, said on her website, nastialiukin.com.

Two and a half years after Nastia was born, her parents moved the family to New Orleans, Louisiana, where they got jobs teaching gymnastics. Her parents didn't speak any English, and because they couldn't afford a babysitter, they brought Nastia to the gym while they taught. Nastia absolutely adored playing at the gym, and she was a natural on all of the equipment. In no time, little Nastia started copying what she saw the other children doing during their classes. She even began to mimic some of their floor routines. "I was always running around and on the bars," says Nastia on her website. "That's kind of how I got started." Nastia's parents took notice. Her father—who is now her coach—told the *Associated Press*, "When she's just playing, and she does it better than your students . . . If God gives you [talent], you're not meant to take it away." And that's how Nastia's life as a gymnast began.

When Nastia was four years old, her family moved to Parker, Texas, and her parents opened their very own gym, the World Olympic Gymnastics Academy (WOGA), along with friend and fellow gymnast Evgeny

Marchenko in nearby Plano, Texas. Nastia has trained there with her dad ever since. Nastia started competing earlier than most gymnasts, at age six. She doesn't remember much about her first competition—except that she was really late. "I missed the whole entire warm-up," Nastia told roadtobeijing.org. "We came in right as they were marching to their first event." But one little tardy arrival wasn't going to get in Nastia's way. She advanced quickly, and just six years later, when she was twelve, Nastia became a member of the U.S. women's gymnastics team at the junior international elite level.

## Going Elite

Nastia made her first big splash as an elite gymnast at the 2002 U.S. Classic, where she finished in third place all-around. From that point on, there was no stopping her. She was undefeated in competition for her last two years as a junior team member, winning first all-around and the individual gold on beam, bars, and floor at the National Championships. Talk about sweeping the competition!

Unfortunately for Nastia, she was a little too young to go to the 2004 Olympics in Athens, Greece. An athlete has to turn at least sixteen during the year of the Olympic Games to be eligible. Nastia was just fourteen. Most gymnastics insiders agreed that had she been old enough, Nastia would have been a sure thing to make the Olympic team that year. Luckily, Nastia took her ineligibility in stride. As she told *International Gymnast* magazine online, "I don't really think about it. I just try to do my job and support my teammates trying to go for Athens, and do my thing."

Nastia was also able to watch one of her closest friends, Carly Patterson, win all-around gold at Athens. Carly trained at Nastia's parents' gym, WOGA, under Evgeny Marchenko, and she has always been supportive of Nastia, often cheering her on at major competitions. Carly's big win gave Nastia something to aspire to. "It was definitely a very good experience to train with her so many years, to see what it took to get all the way up to the top, and I was really thankful that I was able to see that . . . She always gave one hundred percent in the gym." These days, Carly is probably very proud of her younger friend's accomplishments, too.

## Making History

Nastia did get to make a special appearance during the Olympics in an Adidas commercial starring herself and Nadia Comaneci. The commercial featured footage of Nadia's historic perfect-ten performance on the uneven bars at the 1976 Olympics spliced with footage of Nastia performing on bars, her signature event, and was aired during the televised broadcast of the Olympic Games. The effect was that it looked like the two women were performing on the same set of bars at the same time. "I think she's a phenomenon," Nadia later said, to the *Atlanta Journal-Constitution*, of Nastia. "She's unbelievably determined. She wants it."

Nastia set out to make some history herself at the U.S. Classic later that year. She won first all-around and became the first American gymnast to ever attempt a quadruple twist in her floor exercise. She performed it flawlessly and the crowd loved it! She told *International Gymnast*, "I am so glad I did the quad today. It felt great. I got it out of my system and now I know I can do it. It's a lot different doing it in competition than in practice because there is more pressure." Nastia is not the only member of her family to perform a never-before-seen stunt in a floor exercise competition—her father was the first gymnast to ever perform the triple back salto, or somersault.

Nastia also won her third consecutive national all-around title at the 2005 National Championships. She was finally ready for the world stage, and at the 2005 World Championships in Melbourne, Australia, she proved it, winning the gold medal on the uneven bars and balance beam. She came in second all-around, only 0.001 behind teammate Chellsie Memmel. "I feel like all the hard work has paid off when I hear that, when people announce my name with two-time World Champion next to it," Nastia told roadtobeijing.org.

## Media Darling

2005 wasn't just a year of big performances in

competition—Nastia also found time to perform a part in the film *Stick It!*, a movie about gymnastics in which she played herself. Nastia told the United States Olympic Committee, "They wanted me to do a big role, but it was right during competition season. I couldn't do it, so they asked me to do it for over the weekend, so I was there for three days. It was really fun, and it was a great experience." Nastia loved being on set. Getting the chance to act really inspired her. After she's finished with gymnastics, Nastia has said she'd like to pursue a career in acting.

Nastia had another exciting year in 2006, when she placed first all-around at the American Cup, the Pacific Alliance Championships, and the National Championships. But the winning streak ended when Nastia injured her right ankle in October during a practice jump—right before the World Championships in Aarhus, Denmark. At Worlds, Nastia still managed to finish second place in bars, but the U.S. team was disappointed when they came in second place, losing the gold to China. Nastia had to take off the better part of a year to have her ankle operated on and to recuperate. "I was really upset when it happened," Nastia told the United States Olympic Committee. "I pretty much thought I wasn't going to be able to compete at all, but every day it got a little bit better." Martha Karolyi told WFAA.com, "It's a pretty sensitive issue. Usually her body type—beautiful, long, tall, lean—her body is not as sturdy as a stockier gymnast . . . She's a little bit on the fragile side." At five feet, two inches tall, Nastia has her mother's ballerina-like build instead of the short, muscular build of her dad. Martha added, "She will come back and she will be excellent."

Ankle injury aside, *Newsweek* believed that Nastia was sure to make headlines again soon. In December 2006, the magazine named her one of the Top 20 People to Watch in its annual "Who's Next?" issue. "I was really excited when I found out. I knew I was doing an interview and a photo shoot, but when my agent actually told me what it was for, I was very excited and I couldn't believe it," said Nastia to usolympicteam.com. "It's a really big honor to be picked . . . and to be the only female athlete made it even more exciting."

## Student Athlete

While she was still recovering in May 2007, Nastia, an honor-roll student, graduated from Spring Creek Academy. She also released a line of pink gymnastics equipment with American Athletic, Inc. The line includes balance beams, mats, and a handstand bar, all with Nastia's signature on them. By July, Nastia had recovered and was competing again. She made a good showing at the Pan American Games, where she placed second in the uneven bars and balance beam.

When the National Championships came around, Nastia was ready to show everyone she still had it.

"I just feel like a lot of people have started to count me out because I've been out for a full year," she told WFAA.com. "I just want to prove to everyone, even if I don't win, I'm still in the running. And with time, I can get stronger." She did prove herself, managing to achieve an impressive first place in the uneven bars for the third year in a row. She also got second place on balance beam and third place all-around. It was official—Nastia Liukin was back. Later that year, Nastia was able to help the U.S. team win gold at the World Championships, winning the world title on the balance beam, second in the uneven bars, and fifth all-around. Not too shabby! The wispy blond girl from Texas brought her total world medal count to nine, matching Shannon Miller's record for a U.S. gymnast.

After Worlds, in January 2008, eighteen-year-old Nastia began college at Southern Methodist University in Dallas, Texas, studying international business. It was the perfect college for Nastia because it was close to home so she could continue training with her father. But after a few classes at SMU, she decided to take some time off to focus on the Olympics and come back to school once the Olympics are over.

## Olympic Preparation

Although Nastia was training constantly in the months leading up to the Olympic Trials—even squeezing in a win at the 2008 American Cup—she still found time for some fun stuff. Early in 2008, she posed for the most famous fashion magazine in the world, *Vogue*. Then, during a photo shoot for *Glamour* magazine, a photographer snapped pictures of her in a chic Miu Miu dress while on the uneven bars! She also had a photo session and interview with *Sports Illustrated for Kids*, and she got her picture taken for the cover of a gymnastics video game. But Nastia was as focused as ever, knowing the Olympics were just a few months away. "Every single training counts," Nastia said to the *Dallas Morning News*. "You can't just go in there and not give it your all one day. It's going to catch up to you."

And as Nastia has proven, she can accomplish anything she puts her mind to. "Always set goals for yourself and work towards them, because if you don't set goals for yourself, you don't really know what you are working towards," Nastia told roadtobeijing.org. "Just never give up, especially on those days that are hard and you don't feel like waking up early and going to a gym. Those days that you are tired, they will make you feel stronger. You have to work hard to accomplish your goals." And it's clear that for Nastia, all of her hard work is going to continue to pay off in gymnastics success.

# ALICIA SACRAMONE

**Full Name:** Alicia Marie Sacramone
**Date of Birth:** December 3, 1987
**Hometown:** Winchester, Massachusetts
**Eye Color:** Brown
**Hair Color**: Dark blond
**Favorite Events:** Floor exercise and vault
**Senior Elite Medals:**

2007 World Championships: 1st-Team; 2nd-FX; 3rd-VT

2007 Visa Championships: 1st-VT; 3rd-BB, FX

2007 U.S. Classic: 1st-VT, BB, FX

2006 World Championships: 2nd-Team, VT

2006 World Cup: 2nd-VT

2006 Visa Championships: 1st-VT, FX(T); 5th-AA; 6th-BB;
    8th-UB

2006 U.S. Classic: 1st-VT, FX; 2nd-BB; 3rd-AA

2005 World Championships: 1st-FX; 3rd-VT

2005 Pan American Championships: 1st-Team, VT, FX;
    5th-AA

2005 World Cup, France: 1st-VT; 6th-FX

2005 World Cup, Belgium: 1st-VT, FX

2005 USA/GBR: 1st-Team, VT, FX(T); 2nd-BB

2005 Visa Championships: 1st-VT, FX; 3rd-BB; 4th-AA

2005 U.S. Classic: 1st-FX; 3rd-AA, VT; 4th-BB

2005 American Cup: 1st-VT; 2nd-FX

2004 World Cup Final, Great Britain: 1st-VT

2004 World Cup, Belgium: 2nd-VT; 4th-FX

2004 Pan American Individual Event Championships:
    1st-VT, FX

2004 Pacific Alliance Championships: 1st-Team, VT

2004 Visa Championships: 2nd-VT

2004 American Classic: 1st-FX; 4th-AA; 5th-VT, BB

2004 Podium Meet: 1st-Team, VT, FX; 2nd-AA, BB

## Born Performer

Alicia Marie Sacramone is just plain fun to watch with her spunky attitude and flashy routines. She's got a real flair for entertaining. So it's no surprise that Alicia is a crowd favorite, wowing audiences and judges alike with her dynamic performances.

Alicia was born on December 3, 1987, in Boston, Massachusetts, and grew up in nearby Winchester with her parents and older brother, Jonathan. Her mother is a salon owner and her father is an orthodontist, so it's no wonder Alicia is super-photogenic, with her perfectly styled blond hair and toothy white smile! Alicia loved performing from a very early age. She began taking dance classes when she was three, and she kept on dancing for five more years until someone saw her doing cartwheels at a local mall and suggested she take up gymnastics. "I think [dance] really helped for my expression and everything," Alicia told *Inside Gymnastics*. "And I think part of it is natural. I really like to perform for people. I think it's fun."

Alicia is known for being outgoing and outspoken,

and her bubbly personality really shines through in competition. She says she gets her attitude from her family. "I come from an Italian family who are all very boisterous and blunt," she told *Inside Gymnastics*. "They say what they want and mean what they say. I've always felt comfortable expressing my feelings because that's how I was brought up. I've learned to keep my mouth shut when the time isn't right to voice my opinion, but when I'm asked a question, I feel it's only right to answer honestly even if my response isn't what people expect to hear." In competition, as in day-to-day life, Alicia doesn't hold anything back. She gives gymnastics her all. Her coaches, Mihai and Silvia Brestyan, who have coached her since she was eight, helped Alicia on her quick rise to becoming an elite gymnast on the U.S. junior team by the age of fifteen in 2002.

## Under Pressure

In 2004, five-foot-tall Alicia, who is strongest in vault and floor exercise, made it to the senior level, competing at the 2004 Pacific Alliance Championships in Hawaii. She got her first senior medal at that competition when she won first place on the vault. She then went on to win several more first-place medals that year at both the national and international level. At the time, Alicia looked like a strong contender to go to the 2004 Athens Olympics, but the pressure of the Olympic Trials proved to be too much for her. Alicia fell and made other mistakes during all of her routines, and she didn't come close to qualifying. National team coordinator Martha Karolyi famously said at the time that she was "through" with Alicia after that. And to make matters worse, Alicia found out she had injured her back at the trials. She had a bulging disk and had to wear a back brace while watching her teammates compete in Athens from home. "It was devastating coming so close to your dream and then falling short," Alicia told *Inside Gymnastics*. "It was one of the hardest things to deal with, to work so hard for something and then watch your chances slip away."

But the disappointment didn't hold her back for long. "Once my back was healed I [found] my love for gymnastics [again] and was ready to go." She spent the summer of 2004 training with her coach, Mihai, improving her consistency, strength, and her mental toughness. All of Alicia's hard work paid off when she went to the World Cup finals in 2005, winning gold in the vault. From that point on, it was win after win for Alicia. She placed first on vault again and second on floor at the American Cup, and at the National Championships she came in first on vault and floor. The World Championships were next. And if anyone still doubted Alicia's talent and ability to perform under pressure, they learned their lesson then, when she became world champion in the floor exercise and won the bronze on vault. Alicia was on a roll. USA

Gymnastics even named this sassy gymnast the 2005 Sportswoman of the Year.

## International Frustration

Alicia continued to perform well in 2006, placing first in vault and floor at both the U.S. Classic and the National Championships. And even though she injured her left knee during Nationals and had to have surgery, Alicia recovered and kept on going. Before long, it was World Championships time again. But this time, Alicia wouldn't be so happy about her performance. Alicia didn't get a chance to defend her world champion title in the floor routine. She didn't even qualify for the event because the judges deducted half a point for a pause between dance movements. The deduction seemed unfair, especially considering that Alicia had been performing this routine prior to the Worlds and had never been docked for that pause. Alicia was devastated that she wasn't able to compete in her favorite event. But she took all of her anger and frustration out in a rock-solid performance on vault. She won the silver medal in the event finals, improving her bronze from the previous year. But the United States came in second place to China in the end. "We didn't lose the gold, we won the silver," Alicia told the *Brown Daily Herald*. "But we have to move on from our mistakes and learn from them to assure that they don't happen again."

## Ivy League Alicia

In the meantime, Alicia enrolled in school at Brown University, a prestigious Ivy League college in Providence, Rhode Island. Originally, Alicia wanted to go to the University of California at Los Angeles, but in the end, she decided to stay closer to home and her coach, Mihai. "California was not the place for me," she told the *Providence Journal*. "I'm an East Coast girl." Alicia chose to attend school full time and perform gymnastics on the Brown Bears gymnastics team while continuing to train in Boston with Mihai. Alicia was one busy girl! But at Brown she didn't have to choose college over gymnastics. "It's the perfect situation for what I want to do," she told the *Brown Daily Herald*. Martha Karolyi is certainly impressed, as she told the *Boston Globe*, "If it's possible for Alicia to do it, it would be a good example for everybody. We are losing a lot of girls who think that just because they are going to college, they decline the opportunity to do elite gymnastics."

In her first year, Alicia took classes like art history and Italian literature. She told *USA Today*, "If I was just doing gymnastics, I'd go a little crazy. At least this way, I get a little variety." Alicia got mostly As and Bs her first year, which was pretty incredible considering how jam-packed her gymnastics schedule is! Alicia told the *Providence Journal*, "School always comes first . . . I know I'm not going to be doing gymnastics all my life." In fact, Alicia already has something else in mind. "I am very interested in fashion design, and that is the career path I want to pursue when I am done with gymnastics," she told usolympicteam.com. And she's getting in her practice now—she already designs her own clothes and leotards!

When Alicia started school, people at Brown were curious about her. After all, it's not common to have a world-class gymnast as a classmate. Alicia didn't let it go to her head, though. She told the *Boston Globe*, "Someone said to me, 'Dude, do you know we have this great gymnast [going to school] here?' I'm like, 'Really? That's so cool.'" After her classes each day, Alicia trained with the Brown gymnastics team. She really enjoyed working with them. It was very different from the highly competitive world of elite gymnastics, where the girls were friends one minute and foes on the competition floor the next. "I can relax a little more," Alicia told the *Providence Journal*. "It's a lot more fun and team-oriented. That's not what I'm used to. It's great to have a team behind you. It's rather new for me."

Her teammates and coach at Brown loved having Alicia on the team. Her Brown coach, Sara Carver-Milne, told the *Providence Journal* that the Brown team was a little wary that such an incredible gymnast might act like a diva. But they were pleasantly surprised at how down-to-earth Alicia is. Sara said, "She is so humble and it makes it easy for them. She is not conceited and never brags. She points out her flaws and lets them know that they can do some things she can't." In the fall of 2007, Alicia became the Ivy League champion in every event. On top of all of that, she was driving an hour back and forth from Providence to Boston every single day to practice with Mihai. "I'm not going to lie," she said to *Inside Gymnastics*. "I thought balancing both elite and college gymnastics would be easier. It took a lot of hard work to keep everyone happy."

Ultimately, at the suggestion of Martha Karolyi and Mihai, Alicia decided not to rejoin the Brown team the following year. It was a tough decision for Alicia, who had really loved her college team, but she knew she needed to focus all of her attention on getting to Beijing. Alicia became a professional gymnast in September, meaning she decided to accept payment for working with advertisers and sponsors. Because of this, she can't go back to competing with the Brown team after the Olympics, but Alicia has remained involved with her old teammates as their volunteer assistant coach.

**All-Around Leader**

Alicia put her all into training with Mihai in the following months. "My days spent in the gym are high intensity and grueling on my body," Alicia told *Inside Gymnastics*. "I spend six to seven hours per day in the gym training and another hour or so doing rehab and physical therapy work." But as always for Alicia, with hard work comes rewards. At the 2007 U.S. Classic, she placed first in vault, floor, *and* balance beam, which is not usually her strongest event. She was also national champion in vault for the second year in a row!

At the 2007 World Championships, Alicia was named team captain. Although like a true captain, she rallied behind all the other girls, Alicia wasn't too happy with her own performances on vault and floor— even though she received a bronze and a silver medal respectively in those events. She was so hard on herself that Alicia looked like she was on the verge of tears after her performances. "I knew it wasn't my absolute best," she told *NBC Sports*. "I was so mad. I wanted that gold. I think I just overreacted at the time. Really, it's a blessing to take home a medal of any color." Alicia knew she could have done better on a personal level, but she was ecstatic with the U.S. win. "It didn't hit us [that we had won] until after the medal ceremony," she told *NBC Sports*. "We were on our way back to the hotel, and Shayla tapped me on the shoulder and said, 'Hey Alicia, guess what?' I didn't know what she had to say, so I said, 'What?' and she said, 'We're world champions!'"

## One of a Kind

With a little luck, Alicia will get the opportunity to lead her team to gold in Beijing. And twenty-year-old Alicia thinks she's ready for whatever 2008 brings. "I'm no longer that young and naive gymnast who had little control over her skills and focus like I was in 2004," she told *Inside Gymnastics*. "This time around I know what I want, and I am going for it." In the meantime, she's sure to win over the crowds with her show-stopping, vibrant performances. "Alicia Sacramone is one of a kind," wrote *Inside Gymnastics*. "The perky blonde powerhouse's upbeat attitude, infectious giggle and say-it-like-it-is attitude are about as far from the gymnastics stereotype as you can get." Alicia knows exactly what makes her performances so special. "I put everything I have into every routine," she explained to *Inside Gymnastics*. "I get to show a little bit more of my personality during my floor routine because it is my own personal style that I'm displaying for the crowd to see. I love entertaining people, and I do that best when I'm having fun on the competition floor."

# SAMANTHA PESZEK

**Full Name:** Samantha Peszek
**Nickname:** Sam
**Date of Birth:** December 14, 1991
**Hometown:** McCordsville, Indiana
**Eye Color:** Blue
**Hair Color:** Blond
**Official Website:** www.gym-nerd.com/samantha
**Favorite Event:** Floor exercise
**Best Events:** Floor exercise and vault
**Senior Elite Medals:**

2008 Tyson American Cup: 3rd-AA

2008 Italy-Spain-Poland-USA competition: 1st-Team; 3rd-AA

2007 World Championships: 1st-Team

2007 Pan American Games: 1st-Team

2007 USA vs. Great Britain International Competition:
    1st-Team, FX, VT; 2nd-BB; 3rd-AA

2007 Visa Championships: 7th-AA; 9th-BB; 10th-UB, FX

2006 International Gymnix, Montreal: 1st-AA, VT, BB; 3rd-UB

2005 Mexican International Invitational: 1st-Team, AA, VT,
    FX

## Olympic Inspiration

Growing up, Samantha Peszek was like any other little girl who loved gymnastics. Samantha, or Sam, remembers watching the 1996 Olympics in Atlanta, Georgia, from her home in Indiana as the Magnificent

Seven won the team gold medal and wishing she was up there with them. "I always liked Dominique Moceanu. And the whole [Magnificent] Seven from the 1996 Olympics was a big inspiration," Sam told *Inside Gymnastics*. "I have that on tape and I think it's worn out from me and my sister watching it so much! I would watch it over and over and try to memorize everyone's routine, and I remember acting like I was doing their floor exercise routines! I knew every single one of them! . . . It was really cool what they did."

Born on December 14, 1991, in McCordsville, Indiana, Sam inherited some athletic genes. Her parents were both college athletes at the University of Illinois, where they met. Her father, Ed, played hockey and wrestled. After college, Ed became a hockey coach at Cathedral High School and Sam's mom, Luan, who is now the publications director for USA Gymnastics, was a gymnast. Sam was inspired by her mom, and she began gymnastics at DeVeau's School of Gymnastics in Fishers, Indiana. Sam's younger sister, Jessica, who is three and a half years younger than Sam, is also a gymnast. "I started taking gymnastics when I was two," Sam told *Inside Gymnastics*. "[Eventually,] I went from one day a week to two days to [competitive-level training]." Sam entered her first competition when she was six years old—but she didn't win much at first! She said to *Inside Gymnastics*, "I have my first ever meet on tape. I didn't do very well!"

## Trouble at Home

Along with the help of her coach, Peter Zhao, Sam improved quickly. By the age of nine, she was a member of the TOPs National Team. Several years later, Sam, who is known for completing big tricks and for being a powerful gymnast, won second all-around at the 2004 Junior Olympic National Championships when she was twelve. The same year, Sam became a member of the junior U.S. national team and was set to compete at the U.S. Classic when her family was struck by an emergency. Sam's dad had a mild heart attack and was hospitalized. Sam was going to forgo the competition to stay by her father's side, but her dad told her to go and compete. Ed said to the *Indianapolis Star*, "There was nothing she could do for me, and I was fine. I would have been very disappointed if she didn't go to the meet." Sam went and placed seventh in vault and tenth on floor. Her dad came out of the experience just fine—and he was extremely proud of his oldest daughter.

## Junior Elite

Sam became the youngest member of the junior national team in 2004 and competed at the National Championships. "It was really cool," Sam told the *Noblesville Daily Times*. She added, "I placed third on vault and eighth in the all-around." She also attended her first international competition that year, at the USA vs. Canada meet. "I really like the international [level]. You don't know what to expect [from the competition] because our coaches don't really know their coaches, so you have no way of knowing what is going to happen," Sam said to the *Noblesville Daily Times.*

Sam continued to impress in 2005, winning a spot on the junior national team for the second year in a row. At Nationals, she won seventh all-around. She also won first on vault and second on floor—her two strongest events. Lucky Sam was invited to train that year at the Karolyi ranch in Houston, Texas, where many elites go to practice and to be evaluated by national team coordinator Martha Karolyi. "It's so much fun," Sam told the *Indianapolis Star.* "It is like one of the best places in the whole world to be." She added that training alongside elite-level gymnasts "just makes you want to work harder." Sam's hard work paid off when she attended the 2005 Mexican International Invitational, where she placed first all-around, on vault, and on floor! "It was really cool," she told *Inside Gymnastics.* "I was a little nervous before the competition, but once I got settled in, everything was great."

In 2006, Sam's winning streak continued. She won the all-around, vault, and beam at the International Gymnix. At her third appearance at Junior Nationals, she won all-around bronze as well as the silver on vault and the bronze on bars. Because of her super-strong performance at Nationals, Sam won a spot on the Junior Pan American team. At the Pan Am Championships, Sam won gold on floor and silver on vault, helping the United States to win team gold. Her three teammates each won gold medals, too, sweeping the other events. Sam, always a team player, told *Inside Gymnastics*, "It was really cool how all four of us during event finals got a gold medal . . . I thought it was really neat how we all won gold."

## Competition Ready

Sam's mantra for practicing is that you've got to give it your all—and then some—to see big results. "You should always work hard and give 110 percent all the time. Whenever you have a hard day, just focus on what your goals are and why you are doing it, and understand that all hard work pays off in the end," she told usa-gymnastics.org.

Sam relies on some tried-and-true methods to get relaxed before a competition. "I don't know what I would do if I didn't listen to my iPod before meets," she explained to usa-gymnastics.org. "It helps me get pumped up and calm at the same time. I actually have a playlist titled 'Pump Up' on my iPod." She also has some good luck charms that she brings to meets. "I bring a little red silk bag that has a couple of charms in it. They were given to me for good luck by my family and friends," Sam told usa-gymnastics.org.

## Moving On Up

In 2007, Sam made the big leap from junior elite to senior elite. She started off the year with a bang, winning first on floor at the USA vs. Great Britain International Competition, and first on vault at the American Cup. But then, in the summer of 2007, Sam was injured, straining one of her hip flexors, the muscles in your hips that help you lift your leg at the knee and bend at the waist. Sam was selected to compete at the Pan American Games that year, and she traveled with the team to the event, but because of her injury, she still wasn't ready to compete. Sam told *International Gymnast*, "They told me to rest it a couple of weeks or I would risk pulling it away from the bone. So, I rested it and had about two weeks of full training prior to the Pan Am selection camp. I didn't think I'd make the team because I wasn't fully prepared . . . I was happy to be a part of the team and get such great experience, but I was disappointed that I couldn't do my full difficulty."

At her first Senior National Championships, Sam still wasn't fully recovered, but she was excited just to be there. She told *USA Today*, "I used to come to these meets when I was seven. I would be star-struck. It's just so cool that I can now compete in them myself." Although she had a really bad first round at Nationals, she still managed to come in seventh all-around and she won the chance to compete with the 2007 U.S. World Championship team! Sam was able to compete only in vault because of her injury, but she still had an incredible time at Worlds. "It was an awesome feeling to literally be on top of the world," she said on her official website, gym-nerd.com/samantha. "I honestly don't think I have ever been happier in my entire life. To work so hard for something, and to have it pay off, was truly a dream come true. And to win it with such an amazing group of girls made the victory even sweeter!" Sam also won two honors for her athletic achievements in 2007. She was named the top female athlete of Indiana by the *Indianapolis Star* along with U.S. teammate Bridget Sloan. She was also named TOPs Athlete of the Year!

**Biggest Year Yet**

Finally, 2008 arrived—the year of the Beijing Olympics. "I just remember when I was little, everyone was being like, 'Oh, 2008 is your year. It's the most important. It's the action-packed year,'" Sam told the *Associated Press*. "It finally came, and it just seemed like it's been waiting to come forever." Sam started off the year right with a win at the American Cup, where she placed third all-around. "I hit everything pretty solid," she told the *Indianapolis Star*. "I've been practicing really well. I was just happy it all came together." She added, "It was just a good stepping stone for the Olympic year." Overall, the U.S. women swept the top four all-around slots, with Nastia Liukin in first, Shawn

Johnson in second, and Shayla Worley in fourth—a good sign for the upcoming Olympics.

Sam was also excited to compete alongside three of her World Championships teammates again. "Shayla and I go way back since we met at TOPs camp when we were ten and eleven years old. We roomed together at World Championships and are best friends," Sam told *International Gymnast*. "Nastia is an amazing gymnast and so fun to hang out with, too. Nastia has been around the sport for a long time and is a great role model for all of us. Shawn and I have traveled all over together and have a lot in common." Sam really values being part of a team, as she explained to *Inside Gymnastics*: "I think that it is very important to cheer for your teammates. I'm a really outgoing person, so it's easy for me to be so loud and cheerful for others, and I feel like if I can help them, then they'll help me when I need it. It's all about helping each other and reaching goals . . . The U.S. team is really good about cheering for each other."

## Big Dreams

When Sam's not cheering her teammates on or winning gold medals, she's a pretty regular teenage girl. "Outside of gymnastics I hang out with my friends and go shopping. I have a fetish for purses and shoes! I love them and have a ton," she told usa-gymnastics.org. Sam's love for clothes and accessories might lead to an exciting career once Sam's done competing. "I like to draw and I like to shop and so I don't know, I want to do something with fashion, I think, when I grow up. I've always had an interest in that," she told *Access Hollywood*.

But for now, Sam is happy in the gymnastics limelight. "I definitely love to compete and that's what I love most about gymnastics," she told *Inside Gymnastics*. "I love performing in front of an audience and showing what I can do. I've always been able to [hit] in competition. My coaches sometimes get nervous because I might have a hard time in warm-up, but I tell them I'll be fine in competition and then I can usually go out and hit my routines. I'd much rather be competing than training!" It's probably hard for Sam to imagine, but it's possible that at this Olympics, little girls across the country will be watching her perform on television, mimicking her routines—just like Sam did when she was little. Samantha Peszek is living proof that with some hard work and perseverance, gymnastics dreams really can come true!

# SHAYLA WORLEY

**Full Name:** Shayla Worley

**Date of Birth:** September 2, 1990

**Hometown:** Orlando, Florida

**Hair Color:** Brownish red

**Official Website**: www.shaylaworley.com

**Favorite Event**: Floor exercise

**Senior Elite Medals:**

2008 Tyson American Cup: 4th-AA

2007 World Championships: 1st-Team

2007 USA vs. Great Britain International Competition:
1st-Team, UB; 2nd-AA

2007 Visa Championships: 2nd-AA, UB; 4th-BB, FX

2007 U.S. Classic: 2nd-BB

2006 Tyson American Cup: 2nd-AA

2006 Pacific Alliance Championships: 1st-Team; 2nd-UB

2005 Massilla Gym Cup: 2nd-Team, UB

2005 International Team Challenge: 1st-Team

2005 U.S. Classic: 1st-BB; 4th-AA, UB

2004 USA/Canada: 1st-Team, AA, BB, FX(T), UB

2004 USA/Japan Dual Meet: 1st-Team, BB, UB

2004 American Classic: 3rd-BB; 4th-AA, UB; 8th-VT; 9th-FX

2003 U.S. Classic: 6th-UB; 7th-AA

## Just Like Sis

Shayla Worley didn't get into gymnastics because she wanted to become a world-class gymnast; she started gymnastics because she wanted to be a cheerleader when she grew up. And her big sister, Jolene, was a gymnast. "I wanted to be just like her," five-foot-tall Shayla told usolympicteam.com. "I wanted to copy her and do everything like her. So as soon as I was old enough to start classes, I was at the gym, running around like crazy."

Shayla, born on September 2, 1990, in Orlando, Florida, is the third of four kids. Aside from Jolene, she has a big brother, Clayton, who is the oldest, and a younger brother, Olin. Shayla's mom, Debbie, is a court reporter, and her dad, Lamont, is a rancher. Shayla grew up on the family's farm, just outside Orlando. She joined a toddler gymnastics class at age three at the gym where her sister practiced, the Academy of Elite Gymnastics in Orlando. Shayla trained at that gym for five years until her coaches left. That's when Shayla and her sister moved to Orlando Metro Gymnastics, where Shayla has trained with her coach, Jeff Wood, ever since.

## Dreams of Stardom

Shayla was homeschooled when she was little, and when she wasn't busy with gymnastics, she enjoyed a successful modeling career, strutting her stuff for companies like Lands' End. "I did commercials for Animal Kingdom and Disney and Universal. When I was six, I did a commercial for Ivory Soap and then I did one with Barney! I was also on the side of a bus at

Disney!" she told *Inside Gymnastics*. Shayla modeled until she was eleven or twelve, when she quit so that she could focus more on gymnastics.

Shayla's family took her dreams as seriously as she did, and they bought a second house in Orlando so that she and her sister could be closer to the gym. With the help of her new coach, Shayla was becoming an incredibly graceful, expressive gymnast, and her favorite event was clearly the floor routine. "I love to compete in floor," she told usolympicteam.com. "Just because I love to perform and show off and add some personality."

## Going Elite

Shayla made a big splash when she joined the elite ranks in 2002 at the junior national level. At the 2002 American Challenge, one of the biggest events at the junior national level, Shayla won the all-around! And at the 2002 U.S. Challenge, she won first place on balance beam.

The following year, in 2003, Shayla became a junior international elite gymnast. She made it to the National Championships that year, finishing an impressive fourth at the junior level. In 2004, Shayla won first on the balance beam and uneven bars at the USA vs. Japan meet, and she won the all-around at the USA vs. Canada meet. She also took first place on beam and third all-around at the U.S. Classic, fourth all-around at the American Classic and the Pacific Alliance

Championships, and second all-around at the Junior National Championships! She had such a great year that she was invited to the Junior Pan American Games, but because of a back injury, she couldn't compete.

2005 was a rough year for Shayla as she recovered from her injury. In her final year at the junior level, she fell in her floor routine at the U.S. Classic, placing fourth all-around. At Nationals, she fell on bars but still finished third overall. Still, Shayla kept on progressing through the ranks.

## Big Girls Don't Cry

Shayla began her first year at the senior elite level in 2006. She had an amazing performance at the American Cup, where she came in second all-around behind Nastia Liukin. At the Pacific Alliance Championships, she finished second on bars. But then, Shayla got injured once again. This time, she hurt her hamstring before Nationals and couldn't compete for the rest of 2006. "Originally, I had a torn hamstring," Shayla told *Inside Gymnastics*. "I thought it was healed, and this one day I was vaulting and right as I hurdled, I felt something snap. They thought it was just my scar tissue breaking up. When it didn't feel any better right before Worlds came, I went and got an MRI and they said I had torn deeper muscles . . . Then, it was back to ground zero and start [the recovery process] all over again."

While recovering, Shayla just kept her eyes on the

prize and her attitude upbeat. "You just keep thinking about your goals," Shayla told *International Gymnast*. "You want to be an Olympic champion. You've got to push through these days. These are what make you stronger . . . and shape you as a gymnast." Because of her injury, Shayla was not named to the Worlds team that year. She was devastated. "It was hard," Shayla told *Inside Gymnastics*. "I just kept saying, 'My time will come.'"

Shayla got back in the game in 2007, when the American Cup rolled around. She wasn't expecting to compete, but she received a last-minute phone call the day before the meet. Jana Bieger had injured her ankle, and Shayla was asked to take her spot. Unfortunately, at the meet, Shayla fell on her bars dismount, and she just missed qualifying for the finals. Still, Shayla was happy to be competing again. "It has been a long and aggravating [recovery process], but I'm glad it's finally over," Shayla told *Inside Gymnastics*. "It feels so good to be doing gymnastics again and not be in pain. [I haven't been back to full speed for] too long—probably like a month, maybe." Shayla explained to usolympicteam.com that overcoming her injuries has been one of her biggest challenges. "To have to sit out all that time and miss opportunities, it's really . . . I mean it's kind of motivating in a way, but it's also depressing sort of. And it's hard to get back up after you've been down so long. You feel like you've lost skills, or you aren't as good as you were before."

## Back on Top

But Shayla was better than ever throughout the rest of 2007. She placed second all-around at Nationals behind Shawn Johnson, and that year, she was selected for the World Championships team! Worlds was a very exciting time for Shayla. Her mother, grandmother, and sister all came to Germany to watch her perform, and Shayla got to celebrate her seventeenth birthday on the day the U.S. team qualified for team competition! The announcer at Worlds even came on the loudspeaker to tell the crowd it was Shayla's birthday right before she competed in her first event.

Shayla had a great day, finishing eighth all-around and eighth on beam. But at Worlds, each team can only send two teammates to compete in the individual event finals, and her teammates placed higher than she did. So Shayla didn't get to compete in the individual event finals. She did still get to compete in the team finals, though. And she was a big bundle of nerves before her floor routine. "It was the most scared I've been in my life," Shayla told OrlandoSentinal.com. She had nothing to worry about, though. Shayla put on a solid performance, and the U.S. team snagged the gold. After that win, she told OrlandoSentinal.com, "I'm on top of the world!" In 2008, Shayla kept on performing well at competitions, but she always had Beijing in her thoughts. She told *Inside Gymnastics*, "My ultimate goal is the Olympics. I have to keep in mind that ultimate goal because it's easy to get sidetracked with other things. I have to make sure I stay healthy and make sure my training continues on the right path."

## Behind the Scenes

When Shayla isn't competing, she spends her time training and going to public school at Boone High for part of each day. Her schedule is jam-packed. "I wake up in the morning at about 5:45. I get ready and eat breakfast, and go to the gym from about seven to nine," she told usolympicteam.com. "Then from the gym I change into my school clothes and I go to a public school from 9:30 to 1:15, which includes three periods and lunch. Then I go straight from school to gym at 1:45 to whenever I'm done with gym, which is usually around seven. After gym I ice and stuff, and then I go home, do some homework, eat some dinner, then go to bed." Shayla also takes some online classes to round out her schoolwork, but she isn't exactly a bookworm. "What I like to do is lay out by the pool or shop," she told usolympicteam.com. Shayla is also an animal lover, with seven dogs at home, and she hopes to become a veterinarian one day.

Shayla likes to keep in touch with her big sis, who recently graduated from Eastern Michigan University, where she was on the gymnastics team. Even though Jolene is so far away, they talk on the phone a lot. "It's really nice, and it's good and fun to have someone so close to me who really understands what I do and what I go through," Shayla said to usolympicteam.com. "Same for her, I understand what she goes through. So it's always nice to have someone to talk to and share everything with about gymnastics that knows what it's about." Wherever Shayla's gymnastics career takes her, she can be sure that her big sis, along with the rest of her family, will be cheering her on, and Shayla is sure to make them proud.

# IVANA HONG

**Full Name:** Ivana Hong

**Nickname:** Nana, Lala, Ivie (pronounced "Eevee")

**Date of Birth:** December 11, 1992

**Hometown:** Shrewsbury, Massachusetts

**Height:** 4' 10"

**Eye Color:** Brown

**Hair Color:** Black

**Official Website:** www.sitesbymorgan.com/ivana

**Favorite Event:** Beam

**Senior Elite Medals:**

2007 World Championships: 1st-Team

2007 Pan American Games: 1st-Team; 3rd-AA

2007 Houston International Invitational: 2nd-AA, BB; 3rd-VT

2007 USA vs. Great Britain International Competition:
   1st-Team; 3rd-BB; 5th-AA

2007 Visa Championships: 4th-AA; 5th-BB, FX; 8th-UB

2006 USA/Japan/New Zealand Competition: 1st-Team;
   3rd-AA, BB, FX

2005 Top Gym Competition: 1st-UB, BB; 3rd-AA

2004 American Challenge: 1st-AA, BB, UB; 2nd-VT; 4th-FX

2003 U.S. Challenge: 2nd-AA, BB; 5th-VT; 6th-UB, FX

2003 American Challenge: 1st-UB, BB; 2nd-AA, UB; 3rd-FX;
   7th-VT

2002 U.S. Challenge: 1st-BB; 3rd-AA; 4th-FX; 6th-VT; 9th-UB

## California Girl

Ivana Hong is such a committed gymnast that when she was just twelve years old, she moved 1,600 miles across the country to train with one of the best coaches in the world! That's dedication! She's only fifteen years old now, but you wouldn't know it to watch her compete. This 4' 10" pixie has a maturity that's beyond her years, and she has been training for her Olympic moment all her life.

Ivana was born on December 11, 1992, in Worcester, Massachusetts, and grew up in the nearby town of Shrewsbury, Massachusetts. Her parents, Mike and Michelle, are both Chinese, though they were born in Vietnam. When Ivana was only two, the family moved from Massachusetts to sunny Laguna Hills in Southern California, just a few miles from Laguna Beach. Ivana got started in gymnastics when she was five years old because her mother was looking for a way to keep her daughter occupied while she ran errands. Michelle took Ivana to the nearby National Gymnastics Training Center in Aliso Viejo, California. "My mom wanted to sign me up for some sort of exercise, but we were turned away unless my mom would take the class with me," Ivana told usa-gymnastics.org. "Luckily, she insisted that they let me try. The rest is history." Ivana's new coaches were impressed right away.

By the time Ivana was eight, she participated in the TOPs program, where she scored very high. She also went to summer camp at the ranch of Bela Karolyi, U.S. gymnastics national team coordinator at the time. Ivana even got to travel to Sydney, Australia, to see the gymnastics competition at that year's summer Olympics. Ivana was becoming a serious gymnast, and her parents decided she needed to be with coaches who could take her to the next level, so she began training at a new gym, Gym-Max, in Costa Mesa, California. Two years later, after recovering from elbow surgery, Ivana competed at the U.S. Challenge. It was her first junior elite competition. Nine-year-old Ivana, wearing pigtails, finished third all-around. After her awesome performance, she was invited to National Training Camp, making another trip to the Karolyi ranch in Houston, Texas.

## The Next Level

In 2003, Ivana, whose favorite event is beam, continued to compete as a junior national elite. She finished second at both the American and U.S. Challenges. But by 2004, Ivana realized that though her coaches at Gym-Max had taught her a lot, she needed to train with someone who could push her all the way to the Olympics. Ivana found the perfect coaches at Great American Gymnastics Express, or GAGE, all the way in Blue Springs, Missouri, several states away from California. Al and Armine Fong, who were voted USA Gymnastics' coaches of the year in 2004 and who had coached Terin Humphrey and Courtney McCool to the Athens Olympics that year, were exactly the type of coaches Ivana was looking for. Blue Springs was incredibly far from home in Laguna Hills, but Ivana was willing to do whatever it took to get to the Olympic level. So, while her father stayed to work in California, Ivana, her mother, and her three siblings—older sister Isabelle and younger sister and brother Isadora and Preston—moved to Missouri so Ivana could pursue her dream. "It was a difficult decision, but a very good one," Michelle told the *Examiner*. "We had the choice of any coach or gym in the country and we know we made the right choice."

Al and Armine saw the awesome potential in Ivana right away. "You could tell she was going to be special," Al told the *Examiner*. Ivana was extremely happy at GAGE, too. She said to the *Examiner*, "I like everything about GAGE. I really like the coaches . . . I like my teammates. I like Blue Springs. I really feel at home." In 2004, when she was twelve, Ivana progressed from a national elite to an international elite when she competed at the Top Gymnastics Competition in Belgium. She placed first on the uneven bars and balance beam and finished third all-around. "I wanted to go to my first international meet and have some success, do well, especially on the beam. That's because it's so challenging," she told the *Examiner*. "And I like a challenge." Later in the year, Ivana finished first all-around at the American Challenge. She also came in tenth all-around at the U.S. Classic, where she was the youngest competitor, qualifying her for the Junior National Championships. She didn't make the national team, but people were starting to take notice of this gymnast with perfect form and clean lines in every single event. "Everything she does, she does perfectly," wrote *Inside Gymnastics*.

## Elite Ivana

Ivana continued to learn advanced skills and combinations in all of her events. In 2005, she qualified for Nationals again, finishing eighth all-around. In 2006, she won second on beam at the U.S. Classic and she finished fifth all-around at Nationals, winning the bronze medal on beam. Then in 2007, Ivana made the move from junior international elite to senior international elite at only fourteen years old! Though the rules state a gymnast must be at least sixteen to compete at the senior level, there is an exception. If a gymnast turns fifteen during the year prior to an Olympic year, she may compete at the senior level. That way, if she's going to participate at the Olympics the following year, she will have some senior experience under her belt.

Ivana had broken her knee earlier in the year, but she was fully recovered by the Pan American Games in Brazil, her first big senior competition. Ivana and her American teammates swept the top three spots, with

Shawn Johnson coming in first, Rebecca Bross coming in second, and Ivana placing third. "It's a phenomenal feeling to go 1-2-3," Ivana told the *Examiner*, "and I'm happy that it ended up the way it did." The United States came away from the event with team gold.

After Pan Ams, Ivana went to the National Championships—her first time competing there as a senior. "It's really exciting to be a senior," Ivana told *USA Today*. "I'm just thrilled to be out here with all the world champions and all the top athletes." Ivana won fourth place in the all-around. "I talked to Al Fong after Ivana took fourth . . ." Michelle told the *Examiner*, "and he said all the judges were talking about Ivana's performance. It was all so thrilling for Ivana and our family. We are so proud of her."

**The Pressure's On**

Ivana was then selected to be on the World Championships team. Still fourteen, she was the youngest member of the team. At Worlds in Stuttgart, Germany, the U.S. won team gold. "It was exhilarating and thrilling!" Ivana told usa-gymnastics.org. "No words can describe the feeling of happiness and pride!" After Worlds, it was back to ninth grade at the George F. Baker Freshmen Center, where Ivana is an honor-roll student with a 4.0 GPA. After she's done with school and competing in gymnastics, she would like to become a gymnastics coach. Gymnastics has taught Ivana some important life lessons, and she would love to pass on that knowledge to future gymnasts. "My favorite thing about gymnastics is that it challenges me to do my best under tremendous pressure," Ivana told usa-gymnastics.org.

If Ivana makes the Olympic team, she will be under more pressure than ever before. But she's ready for it. "For as long as I can remember, I've dreamed of being an Olympian," she told the *Examiner*. "It's just so exciting . . . I can't believe it. It's almost like it's happening to someone else and not me." And if 2008 isn't her year, there's always 2012!

# BRIDGET SLOAN

**Full Name:** Bridget Sloan
**Date of Birth:** June 23, 1992
**Hometown:** Pittsboro, Indiana
**Hair Color:** Reddish brown
**Official Website:** www.bridgetsloan.com
**Favorite Event:** Balance beam
**Senior Elite Medals:**

2008 Italy-Spain-Poland-USA competition: 1st-Team

2007 Good Luck Beijing International Tournament: 2nd-FX;
      3rd-AA; 4th-BB; 7th-UB

2007 Toyota Cup: 3rd-UB, FX

2007 World Championships: 1st-Team (reserve athlete)

2007 Visa Championships: 2nd-FX; 5th-AA, UB; 10th-BB

2007 U.S. Classic: 1st-AA; 2nd-UB; 3rd-VT, BB, FX(T)

2007 Houston International Invitational: 3rd-AA

2007 USA vs. Great Britain International Competition:
      1st-Team; 3rd-FX; 6th-AA

2003 U.S. Challenge: 2nd-UB; 5th-AA

## Baby Bridget

If you had asked Bridget Sloan one year ago if she thought she might be going to the Olympics, she would have said, "No way." But the sixteen-year-old from Indiana has taken the elite gymnastics scene by storm, impressing judges with her awesome performances in every event.

Not so long ago, Bridget was just your average little girl, growing up in Pittsboro, Indiana, a small suburban town outside of Indianapolis. Bridget was born on June 23, 1992, in Cincinnati, Ohio, and her parents, Jeff and Mary, moved the family to Indiana shortly after. Bridget is the youngest of four children: she has two big brothers, Kyle and Nathan, and a big sister, Kassie. As the baby of the family Bridget was always restless and clamoring for attention when she was little. When she was four, Bridget's parents enrolled her in gymnastics class. "I was very active as a young child," Bridget told usa-gymnastics.org, "so my parents signed me up in order to channel my energy."

## Quick Climber

Bridget immediately began training with her coach, Marvin Sharp. Marvin saw potential in Bridget from the beginning. He told nbcolympics.com, "I really thought about the elite program and I tried to choose skills and progressions that would take her there." Marvin's plan worked! Seven years of rigorous training later, Bridget joined the U.S. junior national team, impressing Martha Karolyi, national team coordinator. Bridget continued to perform well at the junior level, but in 2007, she was given the chance to move up to the senior level—far sooner than she had expected to. USA Gymnastics, the group that controls elite gymnastics competitions in the United States, told Bridget she could compete at the senior level at the U.S. Classic. It was a tough decision for her and Marvin since she had planned to stay at the junior level for quite a bit longer. But Bridget told *NBC Sports*, "Junior was in my mind, but I thought, why not [try senior]? [They] called me and said, 'We need to know,' so I decided. 'Let's just do this. No turning back now.'"

## Holding Her Own

Bridget quickly showed she could hang with the big girls. She placed first all-around at the U.S. Classic, her first senior-level competition and her first gold all-around title. From there, it was on to the National Championships, where she received the silver medal in floor, qualifying her for the World Championship team, but Bridget didn't actually expect to be chosen as an alternate for the Worlds team. It was a huge honor and responsibility for someone so young. If any of the girls got injured or sick, Bridget would have to perform in her place. She told *NBC Sports*, "Going in, Worlds wasn't even in my plan for [National] Championships. My plan was just to make the national team, since I was just a baby senior and it was only my third Nationals." Bridget hopped on a plane with the rest of the U.S. team and traveled to Stuttgart, Germany. Although she didn't end up competing and only watched her teammates perform from the stands, she was still a part of an amazing experience—bringing home team gold from the World

Championships. She said to usa-gymnastics.org that winning the team gold was "one of the best feelings ever. It was indescribable."

After she got home from Worlds, Bridget began high school at Tri-West High School, where she is an honor-roll student. Her favorite subject is science. A few months later, Bridget was back on her way to another big international competition. But this time, she was going all the way to the site of the 2008 Olympics—Beijing, China. Bridget competed in the special Olympic Test Event there along with fellow U.S. gymnast Chellsie Memmel. This competition allowed gymnasts to see the arena in which they would compete in less than a year. It was a little overwhelming for Bridget to be competing alongside the girls she had looked up to for so long. "When I was standing next to them, I did think, 'Man, I was watching them from the crowd at Worlds, but I tried to keep that under control and think about my routines," she told *NBC Sports*. "But really, it was more about keeping my routines clean in the all-around rather than worry about who was next to me."

Bridget put on a stellar performance at the test event. She even beat veteran teammate Chellsie, who was still recovering from a shoulder injury. "I think I did pretty well," Bridget told *NBC Sports*. "I can do better on bars. It's not my strongest event, but it's coming along." And Bridget liked competing in the National Indoor Stadium. Bridget said to *Inside Gymnastics*, "It's fantastic here [at

the stadium] because you can really feel the crowds."
During the trip, Bridget and Chellsie really bonded. "We
became close on this trip and it was great to spend a long
time with someone who has so much experience," she
said to *NBC Sports*. "She taught me a lot about keeping
calm, and when I was nervous she would hand me my
iPod and say, 'Sit and listen!' because she knew it helped
me. When we had a lot of waiting, she would just talk to
me and keep my mind somewhere else."

## Eyes on the Prize

Bridget knows one thing for sure: If she wants to
make the Olympic team, she'll have to work hard to
prepare. She told *NBC Sports*, "Form is definitely my
main focus. It just goes to show you that being clean
can take you a long way, even if you don't have the big
skills. My routines may not have as much difficulty, but
with good form you can compete with and beat people
with higher difficulty." Bridget may be new to the elite
gymnastics game, but she knows what it takes to get to
the top. And with a little luck and determination, she'll
be helping the U.S. team on their way to the top of the
gold medal podium in Beijing.

# Chapter 5

## America's Next Top Gymnasts

The 2007 World Championship U.S. Women's gymnastics team included some of the nation's finest gymnasts, but there is certainly no guarantee that those girls will be on the 2008 Olympic team. To win one of the coveted Olympic spots, Shawn, Nastia, Alicia, Samantha, Shayla, Ivana, and Bridget will be competing against a whole crop of gymnastics powerhouses, some new and some old competitors who didn't end up on the 2007 World team because of injuries. Every girl at the Olympic Trials will be hungry for a win. Each of these top-notch gymnasts has been training for and dreaming of Olympic gold since they were little, and they won't be giving up without a fight. Here is a little more about these up-and-coming stars:

Samantha Peszek flies through the air in her uneven bar routine.

Shayla Worley hits a pose on the balance beam.

Shawn Johnson leaps through the air.

Nastia Liukin wows the crowd on the balance beam.

Alicia Sacramone performs a
back handspring on beam.

Shawn Johnson, Ivana Hong, Samantha Peszek,
Shayla Worley, Alicia Sacramone, and Nastia Liukin, from le
at the 2007 Gymnastics World Championships.

# CHELLSIE MEMMEL

**Full Name:** Chellsie Marie Memmel
**Nickname:** Chells
**Date of Birth:** June 23, 1988
**Hometown:** West Allis, Wisconsin
**Height**: 5' 2"
**Eye Color:** Blue
**Hair Color:** Dark brown
**Official Website:** www.chellsiememmel.net
**Favorite Event:** Uneven bars
**Senior Elite Medals:**

    2007 Good Luck Beijing International Tournament: 3rd-BB, FX; 5th-AA

    2007 Toyota Cup: 1st-FX; 2nd-BB

    2007 U.S. Classic: 5th-VT

    2006 World Championships: 2nd-Team

    2006 Pacific Alliance Championships: 1st-Team, AA(T), BB; 2nd-FX

    2006 Visa Championships: 3rd-FX; 4th-AA, BB; 5th-UB

    2005 World Championships: 1st-AA; 2nd-UB, BB

    2005 Pan American Championships: 1st-Team, AA, UB, BB

    2005 USA/SUI: 1st-Team, VT; 2nd-UB; 3rd-BB

    2005 USA/GBR: 1st-Team, UB

    2005 American Cup: 1st-UB; 3rd-BB

    2005 Visa Championships: 2nd-AA, UB, BB; 3rd-FX

    2005 U.S. Classic: 2nd-BB; 3rd-UB; 4th-AA; 7th-VT

    2004 World Cup Final: 1st-UB

2004 Pan American Individual Event Championships: 1st-UB, BB

2004 Visa American Cup: 2nd-UB; 3rd-AA, BB

2003 Pan American Games: 1st-Team, AA, UB; 3rd-BB

2003 World Championships: 1st-Team, UB; 6th-BB; 8th-AA

2003 Pacific Challenge (USA/CAN/AUS): 1st-Team, UB

2003 National Championships: 6th-BB; 7th-UB; 10th-AA

2003 American Classic: 1st-UB, BB; 3rd-AA

2002 International Gymnastics Tournament: 1st-Team; 3rd-UB

2002 USA/Belgium: 1st-Team, AA, UB, FX; 2nd-BB; 3rd-VT

2002 USA/Mexico Friendship Competition: 1st-Team; 2nd-FX; 3rd-AA

2002 Podium Meet: 4th-FX; 9th-BB

2000 USA vs. France: 1st-Team; 2nd-AA

2000 Puerto Rico Cup: 1st-AA, BB, FX; 2nd-UB

2000 John Hancock U.S. Gymnastics Championships: 6th-FX

2000 American Classic: 7th-AA

1999 Gymnastics Festival: 1st-AA, UB, BB; 4th-FX

1999 American Challenge: 1st-AA, VT, UB, BB; 2nd-FX

## A Family Affair

Chellsie Marie Memmel is only twenty years old, but with eight years of elite gymnastics under her belt, she's been competing longer than anyone else on the U.S. team. Chellsie has collected more medals than any of her teammates, and she even has a gymnastics move named after her.

Chellsie has been training her entire life to make

her debut at the Olympics. She was born on June 23, 1988, in Milwaukee, Wisconsin, and there was really no question that she would go into gymnastics. Gymnastics is a tradition in the Memmel family. Chellsie's parents, Andrew and Jeanelle, were both former All-American gymnasts in college, and her two little sisters, Mara and Skyler, are gymnasts, too! When Chellsie was only a year old, her parents put her in gymnastics class, just for fun back then. But by the time Chellsie was a toddler, gymnastics began to play a bigger role in her life. She even competed in her first competition around that time. "I was four the first time I competed in the little compulsory competition," Chellsie told roadtobeijing.org. Four years later, when Chellsie was eight, her parents sent her to train with renowned coach Jim Chudy. By that time, Andrew and Jeanelle had opened their own gymnastics facility, M&M Gymnastics, but they felt Chellsie would have a better experience training with a well-known coach. "She was younger, and I wanted to just be the parent," Chellsie's dad told *USA Today*, adding, "Could I do it? And would I disappoint her? Because she did look up to me as a father. I didn't want to disappoint her at two different levels, as a coach and as a parent."

## All-Around Standout

That decision worked out well for everyone. At age eleven, in 1999, Chellsie began competing as an elite gymnast on the junior national team. She burst onto the scene, winning the American Challenge. Then in 2000, she became a junior international elite gymnast and placed first all-around in two international events! Over the next two years, she won several first-place medals and first all-around medals at the national and international level. Though she was sidelined for an entire year in 2001 with a hamstring injury, she was back in 2002, when she placed third at Junior Nationals. In a short amount of time, Chellsie had proved that she could score big points in all four events.

Finally, in 2003, Chellsie made her debut on the senior U.S. team, placing third all-around at two national events, the National Podium Meet and the American Classic. Then she got her first taste of gold at the senior level, placing first all-around at the Pacific Challenge. Unfortunately, after such a strong start on the senior elite circuit, Chellsie badly bruised her foot. Because of her injury, she made a disappointing show at Nationals, placing tenth all-around. That tenth-place finish set her back, and although Chellsie was selected to compete on the Pan American Games team, she didn't make the cut for the 2003 World Championship team.

**Saving Grace**

Chellsie made the best of the situation even though she was disappointed not to be competing at Worlds. She rocked the arena at the Pan Ams, winning gold in the all-around competition. And she won three more medals, snagging team gold, individual gold on uneven bars, and bronze on balance beam! Chellsie's stellar performance proved that she was fully recovered from her injury. The gymnastics world certainly took note, and right after the competition, Chellsie was asked to be the alternate to the 2003 Worlds team. She didn't know it then, but that invitation would give her a big chance to shine a few months later.

When the World Championships in Anaheim, California, rolled around, three of the U.S. World team members were either injured or too sick to compete. Chellsie, as the alternate, had to step in. Chellsie wound up competing in all four events, scoring the highest all-around score of any team member and tying for first place on the uneven bars, her favorite event, with teammate Hollie Vise. "I just love to do it, and things just come pretty naturally to me on it," she told roadtobeijing.org. Thanks to Chellsie, with only five out of six U.S. gymnasts performing at the World Championships, the U.S. team won the gold on their home turf. It was the first time the U.S. team had *ever* won the World Championships! "I thought I'd just be cheering the team on from the sidelines," Chellsie told *USA Today*. "But this is definitely much better."

## Bad Luck

With the team gold and her personal triumphs at

Worlds, Chellsie was officially a star in the gymnastics world. At her first competition after Worlds, the American Cup, she placed third all-around behind Carly Patterson and Courtney McCool. The 2004 Olympics in Athens were coming up after that, and most experts were sure Chellsie would make the team. But it wasn't meant to be that year. Unfortunately, at training camp, Chellsie broke her foot while practicing on beam. Her injury stopped her from competing at the 2004 Nationals. And although she was healed in time for the Olympic selection camp at Martha Karolyi's ranch, she still wasn't back to full strength. Instead, Chellsie wound up an alternate for the 2004 Olympic team, and this time, she didn't get to compete. "I was disappointed at first," Chellsie said to the *Honolulu Star-Bulletin*, "but then I went home and started training to prove to myself that I could do it and to show everyone else that I could compete for the U.S. and do well."

## Daddy's Girl

After the United States won team silver at Athens, Chellsie got back to training, winning the gold on the uneven bars at the 2004 World Cup. 2005 rolled in, and Chellsie decided she needed a change, so she switched coaches. This time, she stayed close to home and began training with her dad! "I really love being coached by my dad. We make a really strong team," Chellsie told WCSN.com. "The communication between us is really good . . . It has been nothing but positive for me." That year, Chellsie won first place on bars and third place on beam at the American Cup and fourth place all-around at the U.S. Classic. Then she won second place all-around behind Nastia Liukin at the U.S. Nationals and took the all-around title at the Pan American Games for the second year in a row.

Chellsie's comeback was complete at the 2005 Worlds in Melbourne, Australia, where Chellsie became the all-around world champion! She won second place on the uneven bars and the balance beam behind Nastia, who won the gold in both events. Still, with solid scores in both floor and vault, Chellsie managed to squeeze just 0.001 points ahead of Nastia to win the all-around title. "It's all very unexpected, to achieve what I have. All I tried to do was hit my routines as best I could for each event, and that's what I did," Chellsie told the *Milwaukee Journal-Sentinel*. Chellsie was the first U.S. woman to win the all-around title at the World Championships since Shannon Miller won it two years in a row in 1993 and 1994. "It's really almost indescribable. It's probably one of the best feelings ever," Chellsie told roadtobeijing.org. "I am still almost kind of speechless to describe it." Following her performance at Worlds, Chellsie was named usatoday.com's U.S. Olympic Athlete of the Week and USA Gymnastics' November Athlete of the Month for 2005.

**Friendly Competition**

Going into the Pacific Alliance Championships in early 2006, with Chellsie as reigning world champion and her teammate Nastia right on her tail, rumors had begun to swirl about a rivalry between the two girls. Chellsie brushed it off, saying to the *Honolulu Star-Bulletin*, "We like competing against each other, especially for the team, because then we both do our best for the U.S." Nastia agreed, telling the *Star-Bulletin*, "We all want to be that one girl standing on the first-place podium with that gold medal around her neck. But we don't take it too far. We stay really good friends. When we get out of the gym, it's just two normal girls talking." As it turned out, Chellsie and Nastia wound up tying for the all-around title at the Pacific Alliance games that year. But unfortunately for Chellsie, her bad luck hit again and she sustained another injury during the competition. This time, it was her shoulder. Chellsie had surgery and was out of competition while she healed. "I lost all my strength in my arm. I couldn't lift it for a month," she told the *Philadelphia Inquirer*.

While she was on the mend, Chellsie graduated from West Allis Central High School, where her favorite subject had been math. Chellsie focused so much on gymnastics, that she wasn't the most outgoing person at school. "I'm a really shy person, actually," she told roadtobeijing.org. After graduation, she decided that she wasn't ready for college quite yet. "We decided to take the year off college and then maybe even the next year so I can concentrate on gymnastics," she told roadtobeijing.com, "and once that's over, I can just put all my effort and energy into school." Chellsie hopes to become a gymnastics coach one day, just like her parents. "I'd still love to be involved with the sport, coaching and helping out in the gym and stuff like that," she told roadtobeijing.org. "But I definitely would like to have another job as well."

## Rocky Road to Recovery

After Chellsie's shoulder recovered, she got back to her rigorous training schedule. "When I am healthy and training for a competition, I will get up and go to the gym around 8:30 and train for a few hours, maybe until 10:30 or 11:00," she told roadtobeijing.org. "Then most likely go to [physical] therapy and do some rehab, then go home and rest a little bit, and then go back around 3:00 or 3:30 and then train until 6:30." All the hard work was worth it for Chellsie when she secured a solid fourth-place all-around finish at Nationals. The next competition was the World Championships in Aarhus, Denmark. She told WCSN.com, "This [World Championships] was the goal. It wasn't my goal to be at my peak performance there [at Nationals]. It's being ready for Worlds right now, and I feel like I am."

But Worlds didn't go as well as Chellsie had hoped. First, Chellsie injured her ankle in training. Then, once the competition began, Chellsie fell on her release from the uneven bars, further injuring her barely healed shoulder. The crowd and the judges were shocked by Chellsie's uncharacteristic fall. As if that wasn't enough, Chellsie almost fell during her beam routine. She saved herself by landing a front tuck with one foot totally off the beam. The United States lost the World Championships to China, their biggest competition. It was a very disappointing competition for Chellsie, whose hopes of defending her all-around title were dashed.

## Back in the Game

Chellsie took it easy in 2007, cutting down a little on training and competitions so that she could fully heal from all of her injuries. She did compete in the U.S. Classic, placing fifth in vault, and in the Toyota Cup in Japan, where she placed first on vault and second on beam. Chellsie also traveled with teammate Bridget Sloan to China to compete in the Good Luck Beijing tournament, which took place at the site of the 2008 Olympic gymnastics competition. There, Chellsie placed fifth all-around and third on beam. "I thought it went great," Chellsie told nbcolympics.com. "It was my first all-around meet in a year [since 2006 Worlds]. It was great to go out and hit all my routines. I'm not all the way back yet . . . My shoulder is good. My ankle is healed . . . It was important to get out there. People haven't seen me in a while, and they can forget that I am training to make an Olympic team and I am on my way back."

In 2008, with her streak of bad luck and injuries behind her, Chellsie is trying to prove that she hasn't lost her footing in the super-competitive world of gymnastics. Since 2004 wasn't her Olympic year, she and her fans are hoping 2008 will be!

# JANA BIEGER

**Full Name:** Jana Bieger
**Date of Birth:** November 12, 1989
**Hometown:** Coconut Creek, FL
**Eye Color:** Blue
**Hair Color:** Brown
**Favorite Events:** All of them!
**Best Events:** Floor and vault
**Senior Elite Medals:**

2008 Italy-Spain-Poland-USA competition: 1st-Team

2007 Visa Championships: 7th-UB; 8th-AA, BB; 11th-FX

2007 U.S. Classic: 1st-UB; 2nd-VT; 7th-BB

2006 World Cup: 1st-UB, FX; 6th-BB

2006 World Championships: 2nd-Team, AA, FX; 5th-UB

2006 Pacific Alliance Championships: 1st-Team, VT, FX;
3rd-AA

2006 World Cup: 1st-VT; 2nd-BB; 3rd-UB

2006 World Cup: 1st-VT; 2nd-BB; 3rd-UB

2006 Visa Championships: 2nd-VT; 3rd-AA, BB; 4th-UB;
5th-FX

2006 U.S. Classic: 2nd-UB; 5th-VT(T); 9th-AA; 10th-BB

2005 Pan American Championships: 1st-Team; 2nd-VT;
3rd-FX; 6th-AA

2005 USA/SUI: 1st-Team; 2nd-AA, BB

2005 USA/GBR: 1st-Team; 2nd-VT; 3rd-AA, BB

2005 Visa Championships: 3rd-AA, VT, UB; 4th-BB; 5th-FX

2005 U.S. Classic: 2nd-AA, UB; 3rd-BB, FX; 6th-VT

108

2004 Olympiad Elite: 1st-Team, VT, UB, FX; 2nd-AA

2003 National Championships: 3rd-VT; 5th-FX; 9th-BB

2003 U.S. Classic: 3rd-VT; 4th-AA, FX; 7th-UB; 9th-BB

2003 Podium Meet: 1st-VT; 2nd-AA; 3rd-BB; 4th-UB; 7th-FX

## The German Gymnast

Jana Bieger burst onto the international gymnastics scene at the 2006 World Championships, where she placed second all-around on floor and on vault. Though this German-born gymnast has recently been plagued by injuries, when she's on, she's *on*. And it doesn't hurt that she has her mom, a three-time Olympian gymnast, as her coach and physical therapist!

Jana was born on November 12, 1989, in Kiel, Germany, to Wolfgang Heiden and Andrea Beiger. Her mother was a three-time Olympic gymnast in the late 1970s and early 1980s, and she also taught gymnastics. When Jana was just two years old, her mom started bringing her into the gym while she taught. "I just played around and did the fun stuff," Jana told the *Palm Beach Post*. Although Jana had lots of fun in the gym, she didn't start taking gymnastics seriously until she was seven. That's when her parents moved the family, including Jana and her brother, Nikolai, to the United States and a new home in Coconut Creek, Florida.

Jana's mother became her coach, and the two began training at American Twisters Gymnastics Academy in Coconut Creek, Florida. Jana and her mother make a great duo. "I love having my mom as my coach," Jana told *USA Today*. "We get along well and we communicate well. She knows me as well as anyone can or anyone would." Jana's relationship with her mom is very special to her. Jana, who is homeschooled, even brings her mom's old stuffed animal, a turquoise dog, to all of her competitions. "I can tell her anything," Jana told the *Washington Post*. "She knows my personality and how I am, so she knows how to coach and train me."

## Mother-Daughter Team

Jana's mother helped Jana become an elite gymnast by 2003, when Jana was thirteen years old. Jana placed third on vault at the Junior National Championships that year. In 2004, she won the all-around bronze and gold on vault at the Junior National Championships. She also made her international debut in the junior division at the Pacific Alliance Championships, where she finished second all-around, winning the gold in vault and the silver on beam. But in November 2004, Jana dislocated her kneecap on the vault. She had to have surgery, and her mom, who is a specialist in physical therapy, helped her daughter to get ready to compete again. "After her surgery, I was there for her twenty-four hours a day in order to build up the right muscles to get back on track again," Andrea told the *Palm Beach Post*.

Jana was ready to compete again in 2005, when she appeared in her first competition as a senior at

Nationals. She made an impressive showing, placing third all-around as well as third on vault and floor! "A lot more people were watching," Jana told the *Palm Beach Post*. "There are cameras everywhere. It feels good to be out there to show your stuff and what you can do. The crowd and the cameras don't bother me much. I don't like it when it's quiet." After her impressive performance at Nationals, Jana was chosen to compete on the 2005 World Championship team in Australia. Jana did well on the bars, but due to a minor injury, she didn't compete in any other events.

## Picking Up Steam

2006 was Jana's best year yet. At the World Cup, she won first on vault, second on beam, and third on bars. At the Pacific Alliance Championships, she won gold on vault and floor, as well as the team gold. At Nationals, she finished third all-around and also won silver on vault and bronze on beam.

Thanks to her stellar performances, Jana was chosen to be on the World Championship team for the second year in a row. But this time, she would really shine. Although Jana made an uncharacteristic fall on vault during team finals, she won the all-around silver and the silver on floor! It was an incredible day for Jana, who also placed fifth on uneven bars while covering for injured teammate Chellsie Memmel. "It feels great [to win the silver medal]," Jana told usolympicteam.com.

"It was wonderful just being out there and representing the United States. I was having so much fun, especially on my beam routine. Before floor, I just thought to myself, 'This is it. Do it the best you can. Go out and hit your floor routine, and what happens, happens.'"

## Getting Ready for the Olympics

At the end of 2006, Jana switched gyms to Park Avenue Gymnastics in Cooper City, Florida, because she and her mom needed more flexible training hours. Then in early 2007, Jana's parents opened their very own gym in Deerfield Beach called Bieger International Gymnastics. While warming up for the 2007 American Cup, Jana was injured once again. She had to have an operation on her foot after she hyperextended it. "[After surgery,] I was out about two or three months, so it took a little bit of time to heal," Jana told *Inside Gymnastics*. While she was recuperating, Jana had the chance to appear on *The Today Show* with teammates Chellsie Memmel and Nastia Liukin. The three each performed a demonstration on beam and had a brief interview with Ann Curry. Afterward, the three girls got to meet a special guest on the show. "We got to meet the *American Idol* winner [Jordin Sparks] . . . [Jordin] said, 'It's so nice to meet you and it's awesome what you guys are doing.'"

Jana began competing again at the U.S. Classic, where she placed first on the uneven bars and second on vault. At the National Championships, she placed eighth all-around. Unfortunately, Jana wasn't well enough to compete at the World Championships, but she has spent a lot of time recuperating, and now she hopes she'll be able to spring the U.S. team to gold in 2008 at the Beijing Olympics! But unlike some other gymnasts, making the Olympic team isn't the end all, be all of Jana's gymnastics career. As her mom says, "The most important thing is for her, every day, to have fun. Regardless of the hard work, she comes with a smile and goes with a smile," she told the *Washington Post*. "There are no tears."

# AMBER TRANI

**Full Name:** Amber Marie Trani

**Nickname:** Rambo or The Hulk

**Date of Birth:** August 4, 1990

**Hometown:** Lansdale, Pennsylvania

**Eye Color:** Brown

**Hair Color:** Dark brown

**Official Website:** www.ambertrani.com

**Favorite Event:** Vault, Floor

**Senior Elite Medals:**

2007 Pan American Games: 1st-Team; 2nd-VT

2007 Houston International Invitational: 1st-VT; 3rd-BB

2007 Gymnix International Tournament: 2nd-Team; 4th-AA;
5th-BB, FX; 6th-UB

2007 Visa Championships: 7th-FX; 11th-AA; 13th-UB; 16th-BB

2006 Visa Championships: 8th-AA, FX; 10th-UB

2006 U.S. Classic: 5th-VT(T); 7th-AA; 8th-UB, FX

## Super-Strong Star

Amber Marie Trani is an all-star on the vault and
floor, where she can really show off her famous strength.
"My family nicknames are Rambo and The Hulk,"
Amber told usa-gymnastics.org. Amber was born on
August 4, 1990, in Lansdale, Pennsylvania. Her mom,
Paula, is a gymnastics coach, and her dad, Glenn, owns
a construction company. Amber also has a younger
sister, Melissa. Like many gymnasts, Amber got her

start in gymnastics because she needed an outlet for her energy. "I had a lot of energy as a toddler," Amber told usa-gymnastics.org, "so my parents thought gymnastics would be a good way to use that energy." She was just two years old!

## Natural Performer

Amber began training at the Parkettes gym, a world-renowned training center for Olympic athletes, when she became an elite gymnast in 2004. Her coaches are Bill and Donna Strauss, Robin Netwall, and Joe Stallone. Amber was homeschooled until she graduated from high school in the spring of 2008. She trains for forty hours a week, with only Saturdays off. That's the same amount of hours an adult with a full-time job works! But for Amber, the hard work is worth it. "My favorite parts about gymnastics are learning new skills and performing in front of a crowd," she told usa-gymnastics.org.

Amber became a junior international elite in 2005, and she traveled to the national gymnastics training center in Houston, Texas, which is run by national team coordinator Martha Karolyi and her husband, former team coordinator Bela. Martha was very impressed with Amber's skills and invited her to compete at National Championships that year. At Nationals, Amber placed second in vault!

Amber's favorite events are the vault and floor exercises, and they're also her best. "That's where I'm the most successful," she told themorningcall.com. "I usually do very well at competition." She also told gymdivas.us that she believes she's best at these events because, "I have a more muscular build. I am a powerful gymnast, which is what you need on those two events."

## Senior Style

In 2006, Amber attended her first competition at the senior level—the U.S. Classic. She placed seventh all-around and tied for fifth place on vault, qualifying her for National Championships. This time, though, she would be competing at the senior level. At Nationals, she placed eighth all-around and on floor, and she placed tenth on the uneven bars.

2007 was another exciting year for Amber. She placed fourth all-around at the Gymnix International Tournament in Montreal, Canada, and first on the vault and third on the beam at the Houston International Invitational. Amber also made the Pan American team in 2007. At the competition in Brazil, she placed second in vault, helping her American teammates to win first place. "My experience in Brazil was amazing!" Amber told gymdivas.us. "I couldn't believe the energy in the crowd. It felt absolutely amazing to come home from my first big international assignment with two medals!" At the 2007 National Championships, Amber placed seventh on the floor and eleventh all-around. Amber believes her strengths will be an asset to the U.S. team in Beijing. "I'm one of the more powerful tumblers and vaulters on the team," she told themorningcall.com.

## College Bound

When she's not in the gym, Amber likes to take it easy. "I love listening to music or going to the movies with my friends," she told gymdivas.us. "But sometimes it's nice to just relax at home and watch TV or go on the Internet." In particular, Amber loves to watch *That '70s Show*, which is often on TV in reruns. She also enjoys reading mystery books, and she's really into music from the sixties and seventies.

In the fall of 2008, after the Olympics are over, Amber is headed for college at the University of Georgia. She was offered a full scholarship to compete as part of the Georgia Bulldogs gymnastics team, one of the best college gymnastics teams in the country. "Georgia was my dream school," she told gymdivas.us. "I always admired how much team spirit they had and how much fun they seemed to be having . . . I knew that was exactly where I wanted to be." Amber is sure to be an all-star on the University of Georgia team. Athens, Georgia, may be a long way from home in Pennsylvania, but if Amber has proven anything, it's that all you need to do is put your mind to something and you can accomplish it. Or, as Amber told usa-gymnastics.org, "Believe in yourself and your ability, and never give up on your dream."

# TESSA PAMA

**Full Name:** Shantessa Leiliani Pama
**Nickname:** Tessa
**Date of Birth:** March 5, 1991
**Hometown:** Kona, Hawaii
**Height:** 4' 7"
**Eye Color:** Brown
**Hair Color:** Brown
**Official Website:** www.got-chalk.com/shantessa
**Favorite Event:** Floor exercise
**Elite Medals:**

2006 Gymnix International: 1st-UB

2006 Pacific Alliance Championships: 1st-UB

2005 Mexican International Invitational: 3rd-AA; 1st-UB

2005 Junior Nationals: 5th-AA

**Beach Angel**

Shantessa Pama, better known as Tessa, was born on the island of Hawaii, in Kona, on March 5, 1991, to proud parents Stacey and Shawn Pama. Tessa has an exotic family history. "I am Hawaiian, Filipino, Chinese, Dutch, Swedish! They just call me a mixed plate!" she said on her website, got-chalk.com/shantessa. Her middle name, Leiliani, is Hawaiian for "angel from heaven," and when she nails her unique, risky routines, she truly seems angelic!

A fan favorite on the gymnastics circuit, Tessa started training when she was seven. She said on her website, "My old coach found me on the beach doing cartwheels and asked me to come to her gym!" She trained with Nanette Turpin at Kona Aerials Hawaii until her family moved. "I moved to California with my mom and stepdad in 1998 to get a better education and so my mom could be close to my grandparents," Tessa told *Backflip Gymnastics Magazine*. "My dad and his family still live in Hawaii. I miss them a lot, but I go out every year to visit them . . . Sometimes I get jealous of my cousins for living in Hawaii." Her dad, a member of the U.S. military, was recently on duty in the war in Iraq. Tessa has plenty of family at home in Dana Point, California, too. "I live with my mom, stepdad [Kui], and my . . . little sister [Kaili]," Tessa said to *Backflip*. Luckily for Tessa, who grew up on the beaches of Hawaii, she was still right by the beach in Southern Cali. "I love to surf," Tessa told *Backflip*.

## Team Player

Once she was settled in her new home, Tessa began training with her current coaches, Howie and Jenny Liang, at legendary GymMax gym. Tessa wowed judges in 2005, when she placed fifth at Junior Nationals and won third all-around and first on bars at the Mexican International Invitational. In 2006, Tessa won gold on the uneven bars as a junior at the Pacific Alliance Championships back in Hawaii. She also won gold on bars at the Gymnix International meet that year.

2007 was Tessa's first year as a senior international elite. Unfortunately, she injured her foot in March and sat out of competition for most of the year. While she was injured, Tessa's fans showed their dedication by voting her to be on the cover of *Inside Gymnastics* magazine! In the interview, Tessa showed that she's a team player. "Bonding with the team is so important, and we are like a family," Tessa told *Inside Gymnastics*. "People seem to think that there is tension between the girls on the team, and there actually isn't any . . . We all know our main goal is to win as a team first." Four-foot-seven Tessa has since recovered from her injury, and she's been back to her regular training schedule with her coaches. Her schedule is hectic, but she still manages to make time for what's important. "I am very lucky to have understanding coaches that work with me on a flexible schedule. They believe school comes first, then gymnastics," Tessa told *Backflip*. "I attend public school from 6:45 A.M. to 12:30 P.M. . . . I usually train from 1:30 P.M. to 6:30 P.M. Monday through Friday . . . Saturdays, I train from 10:30 A.M. to 3:00 P.M."

**Looking Ahead**

Once Tessa graduates from high school, she wants to continue her education by attending college—and competing there, too. "I love college gymnastics!" Tessa said to *Backflip*. "I will definitely be attending college in 2009 and hopefully on scholarship!" Tessa's got big ambitions once she's done competing. She said to *Backflip*, "I have always wanted to be an archaeologist since I was little! I think I would also like to be a teacher. I also want to have a book published . . . I have a long time to think about it, though." In the short term, Tessa is just enjoying performing for her legions of loyal fans!

# ASHLEY PRIESS

**Full Name:** Ashley Priess
**Date of Birth:** March 8, 1990
**Hometown:** Wheaton, Illinois
**Hair Color:** Red
**Favorite Event:** Uneven bars
**Senior Elite Medals:**

2007 Houston International Invitational: 3rd-UB

2006 World Championships: 2nd-Team; 10th-AA

2006 World Cup, Belgium: 2nd-BB; 3rd-FX

2006 World Cup, France: 1st-BB; 2nd-UB

2006 Visa Championships: 5th-BB; 6th-AA, UB, FX

2006 U.S. Classic: 1st-AA(T); 2nd-FX(T); 3rd-UB, BB; 4th-VT

2005 Massilia Gym Cup: 2nd-Team, BB; 7th-AA

2005 USA/GBR: 1st-Team

2005 USA/SUI: 1st-Team

2004 USA/Japan Dual Meet: 1st-Team, FX; 2nd-AA, UB; 3rd-VT

2003 USA/Japan: 1st-Team; 2nd-UB; 3rd-AA, FX

2001 Women's Junior Olympic Level 10 National Championships: 3rd-UB

## Following Her Heroes

Ashley Priess was out of the picture in 2007 with a back injury, but she's back and competing for a slot on the 2008 Olympic team! Ashley was born in Wheaton, Illinois, outside Chicago, on March 8, 1990. She's the daughter of Mel, a sales manager, and Linda. She also has a big sister, Courtney, who was once an elite gymnast, too. "I always wanted to be just like her," Ashley told usa-gymnastics.org. Ashley followed right in her sister's footsteps, starting gymnastics when she was just three and, after several years of hard training, quickly advancing to the elite levels. In 2002, when Ashley first became an elite gymnast, she and her sister moved to Hamilton, Ohio, to train with Mary Lee Tracy at Cincinnati Gymnastics. Mary Lee was famous for having coached several elite gymnasts, including 1996 Olympic team members Amanda Borden and Jaycie Phelps. "We saw her gymnasts on TV, but what really made us want to come was her encouraging atmosphere and attitude," Ashley told *International Gymnast*. "The gym has such a great environment, and it felt like the right place for us."

## Through the Pain

Training with Mary Lee did the trick for Ashley. By 2003, she placed third all-around at the Junior National Championships. In 2004, she made her international debut when she placed third all-around at the Pacific Alliance Championships. She also won the U.S. Classic junior all-around title and placed fourth at the 2004 Junior Nationals.

In 2005, Ashley again won the U.S. Classic. Heading into the Junior Nationals for the third year, she was expected to win. But a nasty fall that sliced open her leg on uneven bars—her favorite event—forced her to withdraw. "I went to re-grip the bar and my hand just slipped down and I fell crooked," Ashley told *International Gymnast*. "It didn't hurt at all. When I fell down, I was like, 'Aw, man, I fell!' I was getting ready to keep going, but then I jumped down and saw my leg, and I kind of freaked out." Ashley had to leave the competition to head straight for the hospital to get forty-five stitches in the gash in her leg. "It really didn't hurt that much," she told *International Gymnast*. "I guess the nerve cells were damaged." Two weeks later, "I was right back up on bars."

## Stepping Up

In 2006, Ashley became a senior elite. "I've been really excited to become a senior, because I feel like I've been a junior for a while," she told *International Gymnast*. That year, she won gold on the balance beam and silver on the uneven bars at the World Cup in France. Then, after placing sixth all-around at Nationals, Ashley was selected to the 2006 World Championship team, where the U.S. won silver. When Chellsie Memmel had to withdraw with a shoulder injury, Ashley had to step in to take her place in the all-around, which she hadn't been planning to compete in. Her coach says Ashley didn't seem too worried about having to step in. "I called her in the morning to tell her she was in," Mary Lee told

*USA Today*. "She called me back and said, 'What time did you say we're going to breakfast?' I asked her if she'd heard a thing I'd told her." Ashley came in tenth all-around!

## Moving Forward

Ashley took a break for the majority of 2007, when she was recovering from a back injury. In the meantime, Ashley attended school at Lakota West High School. She graduated in the spring of 2008. In the fall, she's planning to attend college at the University of Alabama and compete on their gymnastics team, just like her big sister. When she's finished with college, Ashley would like to become an elementary school teacher. In the short term, Ashley's vying for a spot on the Olympic team. Ashley told usa-gymnastics.org, "I love that satisfying feeling at competitions when I've done my very best, and all of my hard work has paid off." Ashley's sure to give her very best attempt at a shot at Beijing!

# CHELSEA DAVIS

**Full Name:** Chelsea Davis
**Date of Birth:** November 2, 1992
**Hometown:** Austin, TX
**Hair Color:** Brown
**Favorite Event:** Balance beam
**Elite Medals:**

2008 Gymnix International: 1st-Team, AA; 2nd-BB; 4th-FX;
5th-UB(T)

2008 Italy-Spain-Poland-USA competition: 6th-AA

2007 Junior Pan American Championships: 1st-Team; 2nd-BB;
3rd-AA (Jr. Div.)

2007 Visa Championships: 4th-AA; 5th-FX; 6th-UB; 8th-BB;
10th-VT(T) (Jr. Div.)

2007 U.S. Classic: 3rd-UB; 8th-BB (Jr. Div.)

2006 U.S. Classic: 4th-VT; 8th-UB (Jr. Div.)

**Big Shoes to Fill**

Chelsea Davis is brand-new to the senior elite level,
but this baby-faced fifteen-year-old is coached by an old
pro, Kim Zmeskal-Burdette, American star of the 1992
Olympics. The year that Kim helped the United States
to team bronze in Barcelona, Chelsea hadn't even been
born yet. It wasn't until late fall of that year—November
2, to be exact—that Chelsea came into the world.

Chelsea began gymnastics when she was four years
old. "Gymnastics was offered at the preschool program

126

I attended," she told usa-gymnastics.org. She currently lives in Austin, Texas, where she trains with coach Kim and her husband, Chris, at the Texas Dreams gymnastics club. Her favorite event is the balance beam. "My favorite things about gymnastics are the relationships I have developed, as well as the sense of accomplishment I feel when I achieve a goal," Chelsea told usa-gymnastics.org.

## International Sensation

Chelsea joined the junior elite ranks in 2006, when she competed at the U.S. Classic, placing fourth on vault and eighth on uneven bars. In 2007, at the next U.S. Classic, Chelsea placed third on beam and eighth on balance beam. She also placed fourth all-around at the Junior National Championships and third all-around at the Junior Pan American Championships. In 2008, Chelsea competed in her first two international competitions, placing sixth all-around at a small Italian competition and first all-around at the Gymnix International.

## Outside of the Gym

When she's not training, Chelsea attends school at AO Academy, where she just finished the ninth grade. Her favorite subject is algebra. In her free time, Chelsea likes to read. She loves the Harry Potter series, and her two favorite TV shows are *Lost* and *Two and a Half Men*.

She enjoys spending time on the lake near her home, Lake Travis, swimming around, kayaking and Jet Skiing, or just relaxing by the water. She loves traditional Texan food, like barbecue and Tex-Mex.

This novice gymnast may be new to the game, but she's got a lot of promise! Perhaps 2008 will take Chelsea's coach, Kim, back to the Olympics. But this time, she won't be one of the best gymnasts in the United States—she'll be coaching one!

# BIANCA FLOHR

**Full Name:** Bianca Renea Flohr
**Nickname:** Bonkers
**Date of Birth**: February 9, 1991
**Hometown:** Beaumont, Texas
**Eye Color:** Brown
**Hair Color:** Brown
**Favorite Event:** Uneven bars
**Senior Elite Medals:**

2007 Pan American Championships: 2nd-BB

2007 American Cup: 4th-AA

## Little Sis to the Rescue!

Bianca Flohr's first gymnastics coach nicknamed her "Bonkers" because when she was learning to do back handsprings, she kept bonking her head on the mat. This elite veteran has come a long way since then! Bianca Renea Flohr was born on February 9, 1991, in Beaumont, Texas, the youngest child to three big brothers. She was enrolled in ballet class when her ballet teacher pulled her aside. The teacher told her that Bianca's brother was very shy in his gymnastics class. She thought if Bianca joined him, he might want to participate some more. Bianca jumped at the chance to help her brother out. Right away, Bianca showed incredible aptitude for gymnastics, and although she was too young to officially enroll, the teacher asked her to join the class anyway.

129

## Moving Around

Bianca's family moved from Texas to Virginia and then finally settled in Creston, Ohio, when Bianca was six. She trained at Flytz gym with Terry Gray, where she performed well in the TOPs program and quickly moved through the Junior Olympics ranks. In 2003, when she was twelve, Bianca made her debut on the junior international elite team. She placed sixth all-around at the junior level at the U.S. Classic and at U.S. Nationals. In 2004, Bianca placed fourth on floor and second on bars at Junior Nationals. She also placed first all-around at the Junior Pan American Games! In 2005, she placed second at Junior Nationals, placing first on bars, her favorite event. She also placed second on beam at Pan Ams.

Sadly, in 2005, Bianca had to leave Flytz gym when the gym could no longer afford to support elite gymnasts. Bianca moved across the state to Cincinnati, Ohio, to train at Cincinnati Gymnastics Academy with Mary Lee Tracy. Mary Lee is famous for having coached two athletes—Amanda Borden and Jaycie Phelps—to the 1996 Olympic Games. In 2006, Bianca had a great year, placing second all-around at the Pacific Alliance Championships and placing first on bars at the U.S. Classic. She had a great fourth trip to Junior Nationals, where she placed second all-around, winning first on bars.

## Beyond the Olympics

2007 was Bianca's first year as a senior elite. She placed fourth at the American Cup and second on beam at Pan Ams. Unfortunately, early in the year, Bianca was injured. She decided to take it easy and step out of the elite spotlight. Instead, she went back to competing at level ten of the Junior Olympics program while training for college gymnastics. Bianca just finished eleventh grade, and her favorite subject is math. Bianca hopes to receive a gymnastics scholarship, and there's really no doubt that she will. She would like to attend the University of Michigan, where a former Flytz friend, Becky Bernard, competes. She is also interested in the University of Georgia, the University of Alabama, and the University of Nebraska—all great gymnastics schools. In the meantime, Bianca has decided to come back to the elite scene and go for the Olympic team. And why not? The girl's got the talent—and competing in the Olympics is a once-in-a-lifetime opportunity!

# GERALEN STACK-EATON

**Full Name**: Geralen Joni Stack-Eaton
**Nickname**: Lou
**Date of Birth**: October 25, 1989
**Hometown:** Abington, Pennsylvania
**Height:** 5' 1"
**Eye Color:** Blue
**Hair Color:** Dark blond
**Favorite Event**: Depends on the day!
**Senior Elite Medals**:

2007 DTB Pokal World Cup: 7th-BB(T)

2007 Visa Championships: 4th-UB; 6th-AA; 7th-BB; 13th-FX

## A Born Natural

Geralen Stack-Eaton has a funny nickname. This talented gymnast from Pennsylvania is simply known to her friends and family as "Lou." But the nickname is actually quite a compliment. "I was given that nickname because I have the same kind of body type as Mary Lou Retton and [as a kid I had] the short haircut," Geralen told PhillyBurbs.com. "It just stuck and I'm just used to it."

Geralen was born in Abington, Pennsylvania, on October 25, 1989. She was the third daughter to her parents, Susan Stack, a music teacher, and Jon Eaton. Geralen's oldest sibling, Melissa, is now a pharmacist. She also has a big brother, who is in college studying to become an engineer. Geralen had a knack for gymnastics from a very young age, with no training whatsoever. "When I was little, my mom said that I was doing splits and cartwheels all by myself and nobody taught me," Geralen says on her website, gymnweb.com/lou. "So, people told my mom to put me in gymnastics."

## Making the National Team

Five-foot-one Geralen now trains with the famous Parkettes gymnastics club based out of Allentown, Pennsylvania. The Parkettes have trained many elite-level and Olympic gymnasts over the years. Geralen's coaches are John Holman, Robin Netwall, and Donna and Bill Strauss—the founders of the Parkettes. Geralen started competing as a junior elite in 2002. She placed nineteenth at the U.S. Classic that year and fifteenth the following year, at the junior level. She also placed seventh at the American Classic and seventh at the Junior National Championships.

## Personal Tragedy

After that, Geralen decided to take a break from competitive gymnastics, which took up most of her free time. "My goal was to make the junior national team then, and I did. After that, I wanted to try some other things," she told PhillyBurbs.com. When she was younger, Geralen also played soccer and loved to swim and dive. Shortly after Geralen decided to take a break from gymnastics, her father tragically passed away. Geralen recently wrote on her website, "My dad would have been fifty this past year [2007], but he died on December 14, 2003, on his birthday, unfortunately. But we are strong and will work through it." Geralen's grief led her back to gymnastics. "My father passed away . . . and I went back to gymnastics in February of 2004. The gym was like a second home for me," she told PhillyBurbs.com. Geralen poured her heart and soul into gymnastics, and she was competing again within a year. In 2005, Geralen placed eighth at the U.S. Classic, and in 2006, she placed seventeenth at the National Championships—her first appearance there as a senior elite. In 2007, she placed tenth at the American Classic. And, perhaps her best senior elite performance of all, she placed sixth at Nationals, finishing fourth on the uneven bars, her best event.

**Paying the Price**

But all these years of gymnastics have led to many injuries. Throughout her gymnastics career, Geralen has broken her left ankle three times and her right ankle once. She has broken her big toe twice, each of her knees, and her tailbone. She has also injured her back. "The one with my back was pretty serious, and I didn't know if I'd be able to come back [to gymnastics]," Geralen said to PhillyBurbs.com. "I was out for six months when it happened in 2005, and I thought I might have to stop coming." Thankfully, Geralen is healthy for the Olympic Trials and selection camp. "[The Olympics is] always on my mind, and I can't not think about it," she said to PhillyBurbs.com. "But it was never something I really thought about too much growing up. I know a lot of kids do, but I really didn't."

## Putting in the Work

For now, Geralen is continuing a rigorous training regimen. "I drive an hour each way from my house every day, Sunday through Friday," she told PhillyBurbs.com. "We start practicing at 8:30 on the morning and go until around 3:30 or 4:00 with an hour break. Then I drive home, eat dinner, and work on my schoolwork. This is what I want to do and I've put a lot into gymnastics." National team coordinator Martha Karolyi has high hopes for Geralen. "As a member of the U.S. National Team, Geralen has established herself as one of the top gymnasts in the country," she told PhillyBurbs.com. "We are excited to see how she progresses."

In the fall, after the Olympics are over, Geralen is headed to college at the University of Alabama, where she'll compete on their gymnastics team. "I'm very excited and can't wait to go!" she wrote on her website. Geralen wants to study to become a meteorologist one day. In her free time, Geralen loves to sing, dance, and cook. She also loves watching *Heroes*, *SpongeBob SquarePants*, and *Gossip Girl*. She likes the Gossip Girl book series, too, and she likes listening to hip-hop artists like Kanye West and 50 Cent.

So will "Lou" follow in her namesake's footsteps and make the cut for the 2008 Olympic team? Whether she does or not, this eighteen-year-old gymnast has a bright future ahead!

# NATASHA KELLEY

**Full Name:** Natasha Kelley
**Date of Birth:** January 1, 1990
**Hometown:** Baton Rouge, Louisiana
**Hair Color:** Brown
**Favorite Event**: Balance beam
**Senior Elite Medals:**

2007 Grand Prix: 5th-BB(T)

2007 Houston International Invitational: 1st-AA, BB, FX, UB;
   2nd-VT

2007 Tyson American Cup: 2nd-AA

2007 USA vs. Great Britain International Competition:
   1st-Team; 2nd-UB; 4th-AA; 6th-VT

2007 Visa Championships: 6th-BB; 9th-UB; 10th-AA; 16th-FX

2007 U.S. Classic: 5th-UB

2006 World Championships: 2nd-Team(T); 7th-FX

2006 World Cup: 3rd-FX; 4th-VT; 6th-UB

2006 Visa Championships: 2nd-AA, UB, BB; 4th-FX

2006 U.S. Classic: 1st-AA(T), UB; 2nd-VT; 4th-BB, FX

2005 Pan American Championships: Team Alternate

2005 Junior Gymnastics Competition: 1st-AA, BB; 2nd-VT,
   UB, FX

2005 International Team Challenge: 1st-Team, UB, BB;
   2nd-VT, FX

2004 Pan American Individual Event Championships: 2nd-BB

2004 USA/Canada: 1st-Team; 2nd-VT; 3rd-AA, BB, FX

2004 Olympiad Elite: 1st-Team, AA, BB; 2nd-FX; 3rd-VT; 4th-UB

2004 Junior Pan American Championships: 1st-Team, BB, VT; 3rd-AA

2004 Podium Meet: 1st-UB; 3rd-AA; 5th-VT

2001 National Gymfest: 3rd-AA

## All-Around Athlete

Unlike many gymnasts, who are strongest in one or two events but weaker in the others, Natasha Kelley is good at everything. "I think my strength is my consistency and that I consider myself an all-around gymnast. I don't really have a weak event," Natasha told usa-gymnastics.org. It doesn't hurt that Natasha has been training since a very young age. Born on New Year's Day, 1990, in Baton Rouge, Louisiana, Natasha had endless amounts of energy. "I was flipping all over the house!" she said on her website, natashakelley.com. Her mom, Peggy, who works for an oil company, took Natasha to a local gymnastics center. "I was enrolled in a mom and tot class at age three," Natasha told usa-gymnastics.org.

## Real Commitment

Natasha quickly began taking classes on her own, and she progressed rapidly. She made the TOPs National Team at the age of ten, and she qualified for the Junior Olympic Nationals at the age of eleven. When she was twelve, Natasha moved to Katy, Texas, so she could train with a coach who could get her to the elite levels and, possibly, the Olympics. Her mom and little brother, Benji, came along while her father, Troy, a real estate agent, stayed back in Baton Rouge.

Natasha began training with coaches Dan and Ashly Baker at Stars Gymnastics in Houston, Texas. Her mom told usa-gymnastics.org, "We knew that for Natasha to reach her dreams in gymnastics, we needed to be in a gym experienced with the elite program . . . We're so happy with our decision and the way things turned out." By 2004, Natasha's dreams began to come true when she qualified for the junior international elite team. She went to her first Junior National Championships that year, where she placed seventh all-around. She also placed second on beam at her first international competition, the Pan American Championships.

But in 2005, she broke her hand at a meet and was out for six whole weeks, which is an eternity in the world of gymnastics, where you have to train almost every day to keep up your strength. But as soon as she could, Natasha was back in the gym. "I got out of my cast and I just trained really hard, got everything back and just pushed through it." Not long after her recovery, Natasha won first all-around at Junior Nationals! "This means so much to me," she said on her website. "To be able to come back after breaking my hand . . . I did so much hard work to get back up here, and [to] do all this is really amazing."

## Moving On Up

2006 was Natasha's first year as a senior elite and her best year of competition yet. She tied for first all-around at the U.S. Classic, winning first on the uneven bars and second on vault. Then she came in an impressive second all-around at her first Senior National Championships, just behind Nastia Liukin! She placed second on beam and the uneven bars, and she placed fourth on floor. "It was exciting to finish second at the [National] Championships," she told usa-gymnastics.org. "I was a little disappointed not winning, but I was happy with my performance, so I was still pleased with the result."

Thanks to her awesome performance at Nationals, Natasha qualified for the 2006 World Championship team. She traveled to Aarhus, Denmark, where the competition would take place. "I remember looking at the crowd and thinking, 'Wow, this is so amazing.' We were just all pumped up," she said on her website. Natasha helped the U.S. to a second-place finish and placed seventh on floor. "One of the most exciting moments was competing in the floor finals!" she said on her website.

After Worlds, Natasha was named the 2006 National TOPs Athlete of the Year. When she accepted her award, Natasha gave a speech to TOPs coaches and athletes from around the country, reminding the young gymnasts to "never give up on your dreams."

In 2007, Natasha won the silver medal at the American Cup behind Shawn Johnson, scoring the highest mark of the day on beam with a 16.35. Later that year, Natasha switched gyms, moving to Cypress Gymnastics with coaches Terry and Tamara Walker. She injured her ankle during the course of the year but overcame the injury and placed tenth all-around at Nationals.

## Olympic Training

In 2008, Natasha has been gearing up for the Olympic Trials. "I train double workouts on Monday, Tuesday, Wednesday, and Friday," she told usa-gymnastics.org. "I have one workout on Thursday and Saturday mornings. I also go to spin class on Wednesdays as part of my conditioning." She has signed on with the University of Oklahoma to compete on their gymnastics team beginning in the spring of 2009. She received a full scholarship to the school for her impressive gymnastics skills. Natasha, who was homeschooled for most of her life, wants to teach for a career. "I would like to become a schoolteacher," Natasha told usa-gymnastics.org. Outside of gymnastics, she enjoys being a regular girl. "I love to shop, go to the movies, and hang out with my friends," she told usa-gymnastics.org. She also loves to watch *Dancing with the Stars*!

But when she puts her mind to something—like making the 2008 Olympic team—she is totally focused. "I'm pretty quiet and serious," she told usa-gymnastics.org. "I'm very driven and like to challenge myself, but I like to have fun while I am doing it!" This all-around gymnastics star is sure to give her all in her shot at the Olympics—and with a smile on her face!

# OLIVIA COURTNEY

**Full Name:** Olivia Chauntelle Courtney
**Date of Birth:** March 26, 1992
**Hometown:** Fairfax, Virginia
**Eye Color:** Brown
**Hair Color:** Black
**Favorite Event:** Floor exercise
**Elite Medals:**

2008 Italy-Spain-Poland-USA competition: 1st-Team; 9th-AA

2007 Junior Pan American Championships: 1st-Team; 5th-AA (Jr. Div.)

2007 Visa Championships: 4th-VT(T), UB; 7th-AA; 9th-FX(T); 15th-BB (Jr. Div.)

2007 U.S. Classic: 2nd-VT; 4th-AA (Jr. Div.)

2006 Visa Championships: 18th-AA (Jr. Div.)

## Quick Rise

Olivia Courtney has recently burst onto the elite gymnastics scene, progressing from a junior elite to a senior elite in just two short years. Olivia was born on March 26, 1992, in Fairfax, Virginia, but her family moved to Florida when she was little, and she currently trains at Orlando Metro in Orlando, Florida, with coaches Jeff Wood and Christi Barineau.

Olivia started gymnastics at the age of two. "My sister was a gymnast, and just watching her made me want to do gymnastics!" she told usa-gymnastics.org.

Olivia's favorite event is the floor exercise, and she also puts in solid scores on vault.

**Up for the Challenge**

In 2006, Olivia became a junior elite gymnast. That year, she placed eighteenth all-around at the Junior National Championships. In 2007, she placed fifth all-around at the Junior Pan American Championships and fourth at the Junior U.S. Classic, where she also won silver on vault. Finally, she placed seventh all-around at Junior Nationals, where she tied for fourth on vault. In 2008, Olivia competed in her first senior competition, and placed ninth all-around in the Italian meet! This promising sixteen-year-old is constantly challenging herself to become better, so she's sure to have a long and successful gymnastics career. "My favorite thing about gymnastics is that you can always improve. You can either learn new skills or work on perfecting old ones," she told usa-gymnastics.org.

**Beyond Gymnastics**

Olivia, who just finished her sophomore year at William R. Boone High School in Orlando, loves math. She enjoys shopping and watching her favorite TV show, *One Tree Hill*. Her favorite food is Chinese. If selection camp goes well, Olivia may get to have her fill of authentic Chinese food in Beijing! "My ultimate goal is to be an Olympic team member," Olivia told usa-gymnastics.org. "I also want to earn a full scholarship to a top-ten college." If Olivia keeps moving at the rate she has been, she can accomplish any goals she sets her mind to!

# Chapter 6
## Olympic Style

Gymnasts don't just have to execute amazing, practically perfect routines; they have to dress just right, too! USA Gymnastics and the International Federation of Gymnastics have pretty strict rules when it comes to what a gymnast can wear while she's competing. Gymnasts can even get points deducted from their routine for breaking these rules! Most gymnasts find a way to infuse their competition looks with a little bit of personal style when competing individually. But when it's time to compete for their country, gymnasts adopt a uniform look so that they look like a team. As you'll see during the Beijing Olympics, the gymnastics team will wear matching uniforms—from their hair accessories down to their warm-up suits and leotards.

Traditionally, gymnasts perform in long-sleeved leotards. And although it used to be against the rules, gymnasts can also wear sleeveless leotards in competition. Before the nineties, leotards were made of plain, stretchy materials like polyester, Lycra, or spandex. But more recently, gymnasts have been able to wear more flashy leotards made from cool materials like velvet, mesh, or metallic fabrics. They can even be decorated in rhinestones or other jewels to give them some extra glitz. But leotards can't expose too much skin. They can't be backless or have spaghetti straps, and they also can't ride up too high on the leg. It's against the rules for a gymnast's sports bra or underwear to be exposed. The competition uniform must display the gymnast's country somewhere on it, and each gymnast needs to wear an identifying number on her back so that judges know they are scoring the correct gymnast.

Gymnasts are allowed to wear gymnastics shoes during competition, although most of them choose to go barefoot. Gymnastics shoes are simple ballet-like slippers made of soft leather. They have rubber pads on the heel and toe, and they allow room for the gymnast's foot to bend while she is performing.

While practicing, gymnasts usually wear sleeveless leotards, but since they're not being judged, they can really wear whatever they want during training. Lots of girls will wear bike shorts or leggings with their leotards while practicing.

During a competition's opening, closing, and awards ceremonies, a gymnast will wear her warm-up suit over her leotard. Each team has a matching set of warm-ups, which are usually a jacket and pants set. The jacket zips up the front and has each gymnast's name on the front left side of the jacket and the team name on the back. Many teams will have matching gym bags, sneakers, and T-shirts, too!

Take a look at the U.S. team, and you'll notice that all the girls have hair of a similar, medium length!

That's because a gymnast's hair has to be secured off her face while performing. If it's too short, it won't pull back. If it's too long, their ponytails will whip around distractingly while they perform. There is no hair length requirement for gymnasts, but if her hair is really long, a gymnast should pull it back into a bun. And many gymnastics teams, like the U.S., wear matching scrunchies or hair ties.

When it comes to makeup, less is more. Makeup should be clean and natural during a performance. Many gymnasts will wear subtle lipstick and eye makeup—like eye shadow, eyeliner, and mascara—so that spectators far away can see their facial features. Gymnasts also might wear some light foundation, powder, and blush. Gymnasts can't wear much jewelry. Until 1997, gymnasts could wear necklaces while they competed, but now, they are only allowed to wear one simple pair of small stud earrings.

Sure, the U.S. gymnasts have individual style off the competition floor—but spectators would never know it to see them marching into the arena in Beijing in their head-to-toe matching outfits. These six girls will be dressed as a team, and they're going to go out and go for gold as a team, too! And those watching from home can rest assured that each of these team members has never been prouder to wear the red, white, and blue.

# Chapter 7

## One World, One Dream

What will the American gymnasts find when they get to Beijing? Well, for one thing, they'll find a vibrant culture, bursting with new experiences, rich traditions, and a proud history. "I've never been to China," Shawn Johnson told the *Boston Globe*. "It's supposed to be an amazing country."

In size alone, China is pretty incredible. In terms of population, it's the biggest country in the world, with over 1.3 billion people. By comparison, the U.S. has 300 million people; that's only a quarter of China's population. Beijing itself is the capital city, and it's the second-largest city in the country, with 15 million people, most of whom speak Mandarin Chinese, the national language of China. When the gymnasts arrive in Beijing, they can expect hot, rainy weather. In the summer, Beijing can reach one hundred degrees Fahrenheit. The streets of Beijing are always crowded with people and bicycles, since most people in Beijing use bikes instead of cars to travel short distances.

The city, which is over two thousand years old, is filled with historical sites like the Palace Museum, where Chinese emperors used to live, and Tiananmen Square. This site is home to many of the city's celebrations and events. The gymnasts will be living near the historic center of the city in the Olympic Village, which was constructed specifically for the Beijing Olympics. There the athletes and officials will be able to stick together in a small community. The village is just south of the competition venues, and it includes everything the gymnasts might need during their stay, including dining halls, an entertainment center, a recreational sports area, and a library.

The opening ceremonies will take place at the National Stadium on August 8, 2008 (8/8/08), at 8:00 P.M. Beijing time because eight is a very lucky number in China! The Chinese word for *eight* sounds like the Chinese words for *prosper* and *wealth*. In fact, many Chinese couples choose to get married on August 8 because of the lucky number, and the Chinese government expects the number of couples getting married on 8/8/08 to be even larger than usual!

The National Stadium is a very modern building built just for the Olympics. With its crisscrossing steel beams and unique shape, it has been nicknamed "the Bird's Nest." Aside from the opening ceremony, the events for track and field as well as soccer matches will take place there. The National Stadium seats as many as 91,000 people, and tickets to the opening ceremony were sold for $20,000 apiece! The theme of the ceremony is international harmony, which goes along with the Beijing Olympics slogan "One World, One Dream." There will be lots of performances, and the athletes will all march into the stadium alongside their countries' flag. Then the Olympic flame, which will have traveled 130 days across five continents, will be lit.

Normally, there would be a fifty percent chance of rain this time of year. But the Chinese government is actually using technology to try to ensure that the opening ceremony is rain free! It's a pretty complicated scientific process, but basically, the technology can cause rain clouds to release their precipitation before they arrive at the National Stadium, hopefully ensuring dry weather.

The gymnastics competition will start the day after the opening ceremonies, and it will take place at the National Indoor Stadium. Just like the other Olympic venues, the National Indoor Stadium was built just for the Olympics! The National Indoor Stadium seats 20,000 fans, which is more than most gymnasts have ever performed in front of—and that's not even including the millions of people watching them live on television!

On the last day of the Olympics, August 24, the athletes will walk back into the stadium for the closing ceremony and the extinguishing of the torch. Athletes from all around the world will proudly wear the medals they've won around their necks. Will the American gymnasts march in with the gold?

The U.S. team is certainly one of the strongest teams, but it will be facing some stiff competition. The Chinese are likely to be the U.S.'s biggest threat at the Beijing

Olympics. After all, the Chinese team is competing on their home turf in front of 20,000 cheering Chinese fans. Bela Karolyi says this might work to China's advantage, but it could also be a disadvantage. "The crowd sometimes plays a tremendous role to give you wings and carry you to victory," he told *USA Today*. "At the same time, great teams under the pressure have broken down. It is something we have to [wait to] see. I can't predict that one." Gymnastics experts around the globe are excited for the 2008 Olympics. With so many good teams, the competition is sure to be fiercer than it ever has been before. "The Chinese team is very, very good . . . Women's competition will be very close," Nadia Comaneci told Xinhua News Agency, a Chinese press group. "Of course the best will win. But it's a great advantage to have Olympics in your country. You'll have a lot of support, which is great."

The United States will have to watch out for Cheng Fei, a champion vaulter and winner of five gold medals at Worlds over the past three years. She has said that her goal is to become an all-around threat at Beijing. Other Chinese names to remember are Yilin Yang and Sha Xiao, who placed sixth and seventh all-around at Worlds. Li Shanshan is also excellent on balance beam and Yuyan Jiang is solid on the floor routine. As always, Romania and Russia are also big threats. Romania won team gold at Athens and has some strong up-and-coming gymnasts. At Worlds, Steliana Nistor placed second all-around behind Shawn and placed second on beam behind Nastia. Catalina Ponor already has three Olympic gold medals under her belt from the Athens Games, including the team gold as well as gold on beam and floor. Romanian coach Nicolae Forminte told ESPN, "She's a big success for the team. She is still queen of the beam. I hope she'll still be queen of the beam at the Olympic Games."

Although Russia had a poor showing at Worlds, coming in last in the team finals, the Russians perform consistently well at the Olympics. Possible Russian threats include Yulia Lozhecko, the 2007 European champion on balance beam, and Ksenia Semenova, who beat out Nastia in the uneven bars final. But the American women are aware of the threats, and they've been training hard to take them on in Beijing. One thing's for sure—it's going to be an intense and exciting competition right up until the end, and fans won't want to miss a second of the action!

# Chapter 8

## Gymnastics Online

The Olympics are fast paced and hectic, so to keep up with the U.S. gymnastics team during the Olympic Games in Beijing, just sit down at the computer and click away. There are websites covering it all—scores, statistics, the athletes, and, of course, all of the events. Check them out!

### en.beijing2008.cn

The official website of the Beijing 2008 Olympic Games contains everything from the history of all the sports at the games to the latest news and results during the games. Check in here periodically for updates!

### www.usoc.org

The U.S. Olympic Committee website is the official site of the 2008 U.S. Olympic team. This site will give updates on how your favorite American athletes—gymnasts or otherwise—are doing at the games!

### www.nbcolympics.com

NBC, the official U.S. broadcaster of the Olympic Games, will broadcast the games online! The site will also include all the latest sports updates.

**http://universalsports.nbcsports.com/gymnastics**

For more specific gymnastics coverage, NBC also has a site devoted just to gymnastics at the Olympics!

**www.usa-gymnastics.org**

USA Gymnastics' website has tons of info about gymnasts, events, news, and more. And they even have an online store with cute USA gymnastics gear!

With all of these great sites, no one will have to miss a second of Olympic gymnastics!

# Chapter 9
## Making the Cut: Olympic Trials and Camp

By the time you read this book, the 2008 U.S. Women's Olympic gymnastics team will already have been chosen. The top American gymnasts will have gone through a grueling and complicated selection process that involved two big competitions and a selection camp to win one of the coveted six slots on the team. The selection process is more complicated for the women's gymnastics team than any other team that competes at the Olympics. But the stakes are also much higher. The U.S. Women's Olympic team gets a lot of exposure and its members are offered some of the biggest Olympic endorsement deals, so the competition is fierce.

The first important competition was the 2008 U.S. Championships, also known as Nationals. They were held from June 5–7, 2008, in Boston, Massachusetts, at Boston University's Agganis Arena. Nationals are held every year, and they determine the top gymnasts in the country, but the competition is particularly intense in an Olympic year as the top twelve finishers at Nationals move on to the Olympic Trials. In addition to those twelve gymnasts, injured gymnasts who were not able to compete at Nationals, but still had a decent shot at making the Olympic team, as determined by national team coordinator Martha Karolyi, were also allowed to compete at Trials.

The Olympic Trials were held just two weeks after Nationals. They took place from June 19–22, 2008, in Philadelphia, Pennsylvania, at the Wachovia Center. For most sports, the top-scoring athletes at Olympic Trials automatically get spots on the Olympic team. This used to be the case for gymnastics, meaning that the top six all-around gymnasts went to the Olympics, but in recent years, gymnasts have had to jump an additional hurdle to make the team. Before they can make the Olympic team, they have to be put to the test in front of the ultimate judge—national team coordinator Martha Karolyi—at a special selection camp. Each gymnast's scores and performances at Nationals and the Olympic Trials are used as a jumping-off point for Martha Karolyi and her staff to evaluate her potential for the Olympic team.

On July 16, 2008, the top finishers from Trials competed at the selection camp at the Karolyi ranch outside of Houston, Texas. The Karolyi ranch is a sprawling farm with lots of animals including peacocks, camels, and turkeys, but its main purpose is as a state-of-the-art gymnastics facility. For three days, the gymnasts performed their best routines on each event in front of Martha Karolyi and a small selection committee that chooses the final team.

The selection camp component is somewhat controversial, but it was added to help create the best team possible. The selection team takes into account which gymnasts are consistent performers. One of the top finishers at Trials, for example, may have just had a lucky day, but at selection camp, she will prove she doesn't consistently nail her routines well enough to represent the United States at the Olympics. The selection camp is basically a way of guaranteeing that only the strongest, most reliable gymnasts make the U.S. team.

The selection camp has also allowed the team to accommodate a recent change in scoring at the Olympics. Previously, during team competition, each country could drop its team's lowest score on each event. Five girls would compete in each event, but only the top four highest scores counted. However, starting with the 2004 Athens Olympics, the format changed. Now, for team finals, only three girls from each country compete on each event, and all three scores count. "There is absolutely no place for error," Martha Karolyi told *Time* magazine. "It's a harsh rule and demands one hundred percent consistency." With the change in scoring, it's not necessarily a good thing to put the country's six best all-around gymnasts on the team. For example, the country's top six all-around gymnasts might put up their highest scores on beam, bars, and floor, but there might be an across-the-board weakness on the vault. The new selection process allows the committee to analyze the team's weaknesses and select an event specialist, or a girl who performs consistently well in a specific event—like vault, for example—to fill in any holes. This helps the team score higher overall.

But being judged by Martha Karolyi's watchful eyes is no easy feat. "It's one kind of pressure to perform your best routines in front of ten thousand people," Shawn Johnson said to *Sports Illustrated*, "but it's a different kind of pressure when you have to perform them in front of Martha." After days of competition, the selection committee chose six team members and two alternates, just in case someone gets injured or sick before competition. Which of the gymnasts featured in this book made the cut? You'll just have to tune in on August 8, 2008, to find out!